Harrap's
GERMAN
Grammar

Compiled by
LEXUS
with Peter Meech
and Michael Mitchell

National Textbook Company
4255 West Touhy Avenue
Lincolnwood, Illinois 60646-1975 U.S.A.

First published in Great Britain 1988
by HARRAP BOOKS Ltd
19–23 Ludgate Hill London EC4M 7PD

© *Harrap Books Ltd* 1988

Reprinted 1989

All rights reserved. No part of this
publication may be reproduced in any
form or by any means without the prior
permission of Harrap Books Ltd.

ISBN 0 245-54631-6

Printed in Great Britain by
Richard Clay Ltd, Bungay, Suffolk

INTRODUCTION

This German grammar has been written to meet the needs of those who are learning German and is particularly suited for study at GCSE level. The essential rules of the German language have been explained in terms that are as accessible as possible to all users. Where technical terms have been used then full explanations of these terms have also been supplied. There is also a full glossary of grammatical terminology on pages 9-17. While literary aspects of the German language have not been ignored, the emphasis has been placed squarely on modern spoken German. This grammar, with its wealth of lively and typical illustrations of usage taken from the present-day language, is the ideal study tool for all levels — from the beginner who is starting to come to grips with the German language through to the advanced user who requires a comprehensive and readily accessible work of reference.

Abbreviations used in the text:

acc	accusative
dat	dative
fem	feminine
gen	genitive
masc	masculine
neut	neuter
nom	nominative
pl	plural
sing	singular

CONTENTS

1. GLOSSARY OF GRAMMATICAL TERMS — 9
2. ARTICLES — 18
   - A. The Definite Article — 18
   - B. The Indefinite Article — 24
   - C. *kein* (no, not a, not any) — 27
   - D. *derjenige* and *derselbe* (the one; the same) — 28
   - E. Demonstratives — 30
   - F. The Possessive — 37
3. NOUNS — 39
   - A. Gender — 39
   - B. The Formation of Plurals — 48
   - C. Cases — 53
   - D. The Declension of Nouns — 55
4. ADJECTIVES — 62
   - A. Agreement — 62
   - B. Adjective Endings — 65
   - C. Comparatives and Superlatives — 72
5. ADVERBS — 77
   - A. Formation — 77
   - B. Usage — 80
   - C. Word Order — 81

CONTENTS

	D.	Comparatives and Superlatives	84
6.	**PRONOUNS**		86
	A.	Personal Pronouns	86
	B.	Reflexive Pronouns	91
	C.	Indefinite Pronouns	92
	D.	Uninflected Indefinite Pronouns	95
	E.	Adjectives used as Pronouns	101
	F.	Relative Pronouns	103
	G.	Interrogative Pronouns	107
	H.	The Order of Pronouns	108
7.	**VERBS**		109
	A.	Verb Types and Forms	109
		1. Types of verbs	109
		2. Tenses, moods and voices	110
		3. Verb forms: the conjugation of verbs	111
	B.	Notes on Verb Forms	131
		1. The formation of compound tenses with *haben* or *sein*	131
		2. The order of infinitives and past participles	134
		3. Prefixes	135
	C.	Use of Tenses	137
		1. The present tense	137
		2. The imperfect tense	138
		3. The perfect tense	139

CONTENTS

	4. The pluperfect tense	139
	5. The future and future perfect tenses	139
	6. The passive	140
	7. The imperative	141
	8. The subjunctive	142
	9. The uses of the infinitive	146
	10. The uses of the participles	151
	11. The usage of modal verbs	152
	12. Impersonal verbs	157
	13. Reflexive verbs	159
	14. Verbs taking the dative	162
	15. Verbs with two accusative objects	163
	16. Verbs followed by prepositions	163
	17. List of irregular verbs	166
	D. Conjugation Tables	172
8.	PREPOSITIONS	189
	A. With the Dative Only	189
	B. With the Accusative Only	194
	C. With the Dative or Accusative	197
	D. With the Genitive	207
	E. With the Genitive or Dative	209
9.	CONJUNCTIONS	210
	A. Co-ordinating Conjunctions	210
	B. Subordinating Conjunctions	212

CONTENTS

10.	NUMBERS AND QUANTITY	214
	A. Cardinal Numbers	214
	B. Ordinal Numbers	217
	C. Fractions and Proportions	219
	D. Measurements and Prices	220
11.	EXPRESSIONS OF TIME	221
	A. The Time	221
	B. The Date	223
	C. Idiomatic Expressions	225
12.	THE SENTENCE	228
	A. Word Order	228
	B. Negatives	231
	C. Direct and Indirect Questions	233
	D. Answers ('Yes' and 'No')	237
13.	TRANSLATION PROBLEMS	238
	A. General Translation Problems	238
	B. Specific Translation Problems	242
14.	INDEX	249

1. GLOSSARY OF GRAMMATICAL TERMS

ABSTRACT An abstract noun is one which names not a concrete physical object or a person but a quality or a concept. Examples of abstract nouns are *happiness*, *life*, *length*.

ACCUSATIVE The accusative is the case used when a noun or pronoun (and any related adjective) is the object of a verb, eg in *I love him/this old city* the words *him* and *this old city* are objects and, in German, must be put in the accusative case. It is also used after certain prepositions, eg *für mich (for me)*.

ACTIVE The active form of a verb is the basic form as in *I remember her*. It is normally opposed to the passive form of the verb as in *she will be remembered*.

ADJECTIVAL NOUN An adjectival noun is an adjective used as a noun. For example, the adjective *young* is used as a noun in *the young at heart*.

ADJECTIVE A describing word telling us what something or someone is like (eg *a **small** house*, *the **Royal** Family*, *an **interesting** pastime*).

GLOSSARY

ADVERB — Adverbs are normally used with a verb to add extra information by indicating **how** the action is done (adverbs of manner), **when**, **where** and **with how much intensity** the action is done (adverbs of time, place and intensity), or **to what extent** the action is done (adverbs of quantity). Adverbs may also be used with an adjective or another adverb (eg *a **very** attractive girl*, ***very** well*).

AGREEMENT — In German, words such as adjectives, articles and pronouns are said to agree in number, gender and case with the noun or pronoun they refer to. This means that their form changes according to the **number** of the noun (singular or plural), its **gender** (masculine, feminine or neuter) and its **case** (nominative, accusative, genitive or dative).

APPOSITION — A word or a phrase is said to be in apposition to another when it is placed directly after it without any joining word (eg *Mr Jones, **our bank manager**, rang today*).

ARTICLE — See DEFINITE ARTICLE and INDEFINITE ARTICLE.

AUXILIARY — Auxiliary verbs are used to form compound tenses of other verbs, eg ***have*** in *I **have** seen* or ***will*** in *she **will** go*. The main auxiliary verbs in German are **sein**, **haben** and **werden**.

CARDINAL — Cardinal numbers are numbers such as *one*, *two*, *ten*, *fourteen*, as opposed to **ordinal** numbers (eg *first*, *second*).

CASE — German has four cases (see NOMINATIVE, ACCUSATIVE, GENITIVE AND DATIVE). Each case is indicated by the endings of nouns, adjectives, articles or pronouns.

GLOSSARY

CLAUSE — A clause is a group of words which contains at least a subject and a verb: *he said* is a clause. A clause often contains more than this basic information, eg *he said this to her yesterday*. Sentences can be made up of several clauses, eg *he said / he'd call me / if he were free*. See SENTENCE.

COLLECTIVE — A collective noun is one which names a group of people or things but which is singular in form. Examples of collective nouns are *flock* or *fleet*.

COLLOQUIAL — Colloquial language is the sort of language that can be used in everyday informal conversation but is avoided in formal writing such as legal contracts etc.

COMPARATIVE — The comparative forms of adjectives and adverbs are used to compare two things, persons or actions. In English, *more ... than*, *-er than*, *less ... than* and *as ... as* are used for comparison.

COMPOUND — Compound tenses are verb tenses consisting of more than one element. In German, the compound tenses of a verb are formed by the **auxiliary** verb and the **past participle** and/or **infinitive**: *ich habe gesehen, er ist gekommen, er wird kommen*.

COMPOUND NOUNS — Compound nouns are nouns made up of two or more separate words. English examples are *goalkeeper* or *dinner party*. German compound nouns are normally written as a single word.

CONDITIONAL — This mood is used to describe what someone would do, or something that would happen if a condition were fulfilled (eg *I **would come** if I was well*; *the chair **would have broken** if he had sat on it*).

GLOSSARY

CONJUGATION — The conjugation of a verb is the set of different forms taken in the particular tenses and moods of that verb.

CONJUNCTION — Conjunctions are linking words (eg *and*, *but*, *or*). They may be co-ordinating or subordinating. Co-ordinating conjunctions are words like *und*, *aber*, *oder*; subordinating conjunctions are words like *weil*, *wenn*, *obgleich*.

DATIVE — The dative is the case used in German when a noun or pronoun is the indirect object of a verb. For example, in *ich habe es ihm gegeben* (*I gave it to him*) the word *ihm* is in the dative case. The dative is also used after certain prepositions, eg *mit mir* (*with me*).

DECLENSION — The declension of nouns and adjectives is the name given to the system of endings that they take.

DEFINITE ARTICLE — The definite article is *the* in English and *der*, *die*, *das* etc in German.

DEMONSTRATIVE — Demonstrative adjectives (eg *this*, *that*, *these*) and pronouns (eg *this one*, *that one*) are used to point out a particular person or thing.

DIRECT OBJECT — A noun or a pronoun which in English follows a verb without any linking preposition, eg *I met **a friend***. In German the direct object is always in the accusative case. (Note that in English a preposition is often omitted, eg *I sent him a present* — *him* is equivalent to *to him* — *a present* is the direct object).

ENDING — The ending of a verb is determined by the **person** (1st/2nd/3rd) and **number** (singular/plural) of its subject. In German, nouns also have endings depending on their number and case. See PERSON, NUMBER.

GLOSSARY

EXCLAMATION	Words or phrases used to express surprise, annoyance etc (eg *what!*, *wow!*; *how lucky!*, *what a nice day!*).
FEMININE	See GENDER.
FINITE	The finite verb is the form which has the endings indicating person and tense. It is often opposed to an auxiliary, eg in *I should have told him* the word *told* is the finite verb.
GENDER	The gender of a noun indicates whether the noun is **masculine**, **feminine** or **neuter**. In German, the gender of a noun is not always determined by the sex of what it refers to, eg *das Mädchen (the girl)* is a neuter noun.
GENITIVE	The genitive case is used in German when some form of possession is being expressed, normally equivalent to the English use of the word *of*, eg in the phrase *the colour of the car* the words *of the car* must be in the genitive case in German.
IDIOMATIC	Idiomatic expressions (or idioms), are expressions which cannot normally be translated word for word. For example, *it's raining cats and dogs* is translated by *es regnet Bindfäden*.
IMPERATIVE	A mood used for giving orders (eg *stop!*, *don't go!*) or for making suggestions (eg *let's go*).
INDEFINITE	Indefinite pronouns are words that do not refer to a definite person or thing (eg *each*, *someone*).
INDEFINITE ARTICLE	The indefinite article is *a* in English and *ein*, *eine*, *einen*, *eines*, *einem* in German.

14 GLOSSARY

INDICATIVE The normal form of a verb as in *I like, he came, we are trying*. It is opposed to the subjunctive, conditional and imperative.

INDIRECT OBJECT A pronoun or noun which follows a verb sometimes with a linking preposition (usually *to*), eg *I spoke to **my friend/him**, she gave **him** a kiss*. In German the indirect object takes the dative case.

INFINITIVE The infinitive is the form of the verb as found in dictionaries. Thus *to eat, to finish, to take* are infinitives. In German, all infinitives end in **-n**: *leben, gehen, lächeln, ärgern*.

INTERROGATIVE Interrogative words are used to ask a **question**. This may be a direct question (***when** will you arrive?*) or an indirect question (*I don't know **when** he'll arrive*). See QUESTION.

MASCULINE See GENDER.

MOOD The name given to the four main areas within which a verb is conjugated. See INDICATIVE, SUBJUNCTIVE, CONDITIONAL, IMPERATIVE.

NEUTER See GENDER.

NOMINATIVE The nominative case is the case used when a noun or pronoun (and any related article and adjectives) is the subject of a verb, eg in *the new caretaker speaks German* the words *the new caretaker* must be in the nominative case in German.

NOUN A naming word, which can refer to living creatures, things, places or abstract ideas, eg *postman, cat, shop, passport, life*.

GLOSSARY 15

NUMBER	The number of a noun indicates whether the noun is **singular** or **plural**. A singular noun refers to one single thing or person (eg *boy*, *train*) and a plural noun to several (eg *boys*, *trains*).
OBJECT	See DIRECT OBJECT, INDIRECT OBJECT.
ORDINAL	Ordinal numbers are *first*, *second*, *third*, *fourth* etc. In German, all ordinal numbers end in **-te(r/s)**.
PASSIVE	A verb is used in the passive when the subject of the verb does not perform the action but is subjected to it. In English, the passive is formed with a part of the verb *to be* and the past participle of the verb, eg *he was rewarded*.
PAST PARTICIPLE	The past participle of a verb is the form which is used after *to have* in English, eg *I have **eaten**, I have **said**, you have **tried***.
PERSON	In any tense, there are three persons in the singular (1st: *I* . . . , 2nd: *you* . . . , 3rd: *he/she* . . .), and three in the plural (1st: *we* . . . , 2nd: *you* . . . , 3rd: *they* . . .). See also ENDING.
PERSONAL PRONOUNS	Personal pronouns stand for a noun. In English they are words like *I*, *you*, *he/she/it*, *we*, *they* or *me*, *you*, *him/her/it*, *us*, *them*.
PLURAL	See NUMBER.
POSSESSIVE	Possessives are used to indicate possession or ownership. They are words like *my/mine*, *your/yours*, *our/ours*.
PREPOSITION	Prepositions are words such as *with*, *in*, *to*, *at*. They are normally followed by a noun or a pronoun.

GLOSSARY

PRESENT PARTICIPLE	The present participle is the verb form which ends in **-ing** in English (**-end** in German).
PRONOUN	A word which stands for a noun. The main categories of pronouns are: ★ **Personal pronouns** (eg *you*, *him*, *us*) ★ **Possessive pronouns** (eg *mine*, *yours*, *his*) ★ **Reflexive pronouns** (eg *myself*, *himself*) ★ **Interrogative pronouns** (eg *who?*, *what?*, *which?*) ★ **Relative pronouns** (eg *who*, *which*, *that*) ★ **Demonstrative pronouns** (eg *this*, *that*, *these*) ★ **Indefinite pronouns** (eg *something*, *none*)
QUESTION	There are two question forms: **direct** questions stand on their own and require a question mark at the end (eg *when will he come?*); **indirect** questions are introduced by a clause and require no question mark (eg *I wonder when he will come*).
REFLEXIVE	Reflexive verbs 'reflect' the action back onto the subject (eg *I dressed myself*). They are always found with a reflexive pronoun and are more common in German than in English.
SENTENCE	A sentence is a group of words made up of one or more clauses (see CLAUSE). The end of a sentence is indicated by a punctuation mark (usually a full stop, a question mark or an exclamation mark).
SINGULAR	See NUMBER.
STEM	See VERB STEM.
SUBJECT	The subject of a verb is the noun or pronoun which performs the action. In the sentences *the train left early* and *she bought a record*, *the train* and *she* are the subjects.

GLOSSARY 17

SUBJUNCTIVE
The subjunctive is a verb form which is rarely used in English (eg *if I were you*, *God save the Queen*). It is more common in German.

SUPERLATIVE
The form of an adjective or an adverb which, in English, is marked by *the most ...*, *the -est* or *the least ...*.

TENSE
Verbs are used in tenses, which indicate when an action takes place, eg in the present, the past, the future.

VERB
A 'doing' word, which usually describes an action (eg *to sing*, *to work*, *to watch*). Some verbs describe a state (eg *to be*, *to have*, *to hope*).

VERB STEM
The stem of a verb is its 'basic unit' to which the various endings are added. To find the stem of a German verb remove **-en** or **-n** from the infinitive. The stem of *sagen* is *sag*, the stem of *ärgern* is *ärger*.

VOICE
The two voices of a verb are its active and passive forms.

2. ARTICLES

The form of any article depends on whether the noun following it is masculine, feminine or neuter, whether it is singular or plural and which case it is in.

A. THE DEFINITE ARTICLE

1. Forms

a) The definite article in English has only one form – 'the'.

The definite article in German changes its ending according to the gender and case of the noun, and whether it is singular or plural. For the use of the cases see p 53-8.

	MASCULINE	FEMININE	NEUTER	PLURAL ALL GENDERS
nom	der	die	das	die
acc	den	die	das	die
gen	des	der	des	der
dat	dem	der	dem	den

die Lehrerin kommt später
the teacher's coming later

hier sind die Äpfel
here are the apples

kennst du den Sänger?
do you know the singer?

es steht auf dem Tisch
it's on the table

der Anfang des Liedes
the beginning of the song

sag es den anderen!
tell it to the others

ARTICLES

b) *combined with prepositions*

Some articles can be combined with a preceding preposition, for example **an** + **das** becomes **ans**. In some cases these combined forms are normal in both spoken and written German, in others the combined form is only used in spoken German:

das   **ans, ins;**
spoken German only: **aufs, durchs, fürs, hinters, übers, ums, unters, vors.**

sie ging ans Fenster
she went to the window

es geht ums Überleben
it's a question of survival

dem   **am, beim, im, vom, zum;**
spoken German only: **hinterm, überm, unterm, vorm.**

ich gehe zum Bäcker
I'm going to the baker's

vorm Haus steht ein Baum
there's a tree in front of the house

der   **zur**

er fuhr zur Erholung in den Schwarzwald
he went to the Black Forest on a health cure

The combined forms are sometimes not used if the writer or speaker wishes to emphasise the article:

wo? – ach, in *dem* Wirtshaus
where? – oh, in *that* pub

The combined forms are not normally used if the noun is followed by a relative clause (see p 103-6):

in dem Café, das gestern eröffnet wurde
in the café that opened yesterday

2. **Use**

As in English, the definite article is used to indicate a specific person or thing:

der Zirkus kommt
the circus is coming

die Disco hinter dem Rathaus
the disco behind the town hall

20 ARTICLES

Apart from cases where the usage is similar to English, the definite article is used:

a) *with the names of certain countries and geographical regions, especially ones that are feminine:*

die Tschechoslowakei	**die Türkei**	**die Schweiz**
Czechoslovakia	Turkey	Switzerland
das Elsaß	**der Sudan**	**der Balkan**
Alsace	the Sudan	the Balkans

in der Türkei   **wir fahren in die Schweiz**
in Turkey   we're going to Switzerland

Note: with some countries the article is optional:

(der) Iran   **(der) Irak**   **(der) Libanon**
Iran   Iraq   Lebanon

im/in Iran
in Iran

Note: all geographical names have a definite article if they are preceded by an adjective:

das alte Berlin
old Berlin

except for the adjectives **ganz** and **halb**:

ganz/das ganze Schottland   **halb/das halbe Europa**
the whole of Scotland   half of Europe

b) *generally with abstract nouns:*

für die Freiheit kämpfen
to fight for freedom

nichts geht über die Gesundheit
nothing is more important than health

c) *with activities such as the arts, business, science, sports:*

eine Sendung über die Botanik
a programme about botany

eine Einführung in das Bankwesen
an introduction to banking

die Entwicklung der Chemie
the development of chemistry

die moderne Leichtathletik
modern athletics

ARTICLES 21

Note: there is no article when such words are used for school/university subjects:

wir haben heute Chemie   **Turnen ist mein Lieblingsfach**
we have chemistry today   P.E. is my favourite subject

d) with **Mensch** when it refers to the species:

der Mensch ist ein Gewohnheitstier
man is a creature of habit

e) *with the seasons, months, meals and times of the day:*

der Frühling kommt	**im Mai**	**zum Abendessen**
spring is coming	in May	for dinner
am Abend	**in der Dämmerung**	
in the evening	at twilight	

Note:

i) the article is not used when such words are used with adjectives to form adverb phrases. *Compare:*

im Mai   *and*   **wir ziehen nächsten Mai um**
in May   we're moving next May

ii) the article is not used after **es ist/wird**

es ist schon Tag   **es wird bald Winter**
it's day already   it'll soon be winter

f) as an alternative to **pro** to translate 'per':

150 Kilometer pro/die Stunde
150 kilometres per hour

g) *with parts of the body and clothes where English would use the possessive:*

heb die Hand!   **zieh ihm die Jacke aus!**
raise your hand!   take his jacket off!

die Frau mit dem roten Haar
the woman with red hair

h) *with types of transport, especially after prepositions:*

mit dem Wagen   **mit dem Rad**   **auf dem Schiff**
by car   by bicycle   on board ship

22 ARTICLES

Note: in many expressions with verb + preposition + noun the article used does not correspond to the English equivalent:

zum Stehen kommen **zur Vernunft bringen**
to come to a halt to bring to reason

aus der Mode sein
to be out of fashion

Such expressions must be learnt as a whole.

3. The definite article used as a pronoun

a) The definite article can be used as an alternative to the personal pronoun (see p 86-90); this usage is most common in spoken German and usually occurs when the pronoun occupies the first position in the sentence:

Paul Gruber? der ist mein Freund
Paul Gruber? he's my friend

Paul Gruber? den kenn' ich nicht
Paul Gruber? I don't know him

b) The neuter article, **das**, is used as a demonstrative (translated by the English 'that') to refer back to people, things and whole sentences:

die Frau? das ist meine Mutter
that woman? that's my mother

beeil dich! das ist der Zug
hurry up, that's the train

du fährst mit? das ist vernünftig
you're coming? that's sensible

c) The definite article is used with the relative pronoun for the English construction 'the one/the person' who:

der, der es getan hat, soll sich melden
the one who did it should own up

gib es dem, der es am meisten braucht
give it to the one who needs it most

ARTICLES 23

d) When used as a pronoun, the definite article has separate genitive forms:

MASCULINE	FEMININE	NEUTER	PLURAL ALL GENDERS
dessen	**deren**	**dessen**	**derer**

These forms are relatively uncommon. They are used in sentences of the type in (c) above:

auf Kosten derer, die arbeitslos sind
at the expense of those out of work

e) The genitive forms above, with the difference that the plural is **deren**, are also used as an alternative to the possessives (**mein** = my *etc*) when the possessive itself might be ambiguous. This happens where there are two people to whom the possessive might refer back. Thus in the sentence

'he saw Fiona and her husband'

it is not clear whether it is Fiona's or the subject's husband that is being referred to. The **dessen** forms refer back to the last mentioned person:

sie sah Petra und ihren Mann

here it is unclear whether it is Petra's or her own husband. In:

sie sah Petra und deren Mann

it is clear that she saw Petra and her — Petra's — husband.

B. THE INDEFINITE ARTICLE

1. Forms

The indefinite article in English has only one form - 'a'.

In German the indefinite article changes its ending according to the gender and case of the noun after it. For the use of the cases see p 53-8 above.

	MASCULINE	FEMININE	NEUTER
nom	ein	eine	ein
acc	einen	eine	ein
gen	eines	einer	eines
dat	einem	einer	einem

eine Frau   **hier ist ein Stuhl**   **nimm einen Stuhl!**
a woman   here is a chair   take a chair

die Mutter einer Schülerin
the mother of a schoolgirl

mit einem schweren Hammer
with a heavy hammer

2. Use

a) As in English, the indefinite article is used with nouns for someone or something which is not precisely specified:

hast du eine Zeitung gesehen?
have you seen a newspaper?

ich möchte ein Bier
I would like a beer

b) Unlike English, German omits the indefinite article
   i) before the names of occupations or similar functions when they have no adjective:

   ich möchte Bäcker werden
   I would like to be a baker

but: **sie ist eine bekannte Pilotin**
she is a famous pilot

er ist Vegetarier   **sie ist Katholikin geworden**
he is a vegetarian   she has become a Catholic

ARTICLES

   ii) after **als** = as:

       ich komme als Freund   **sie gilt als ausgezeichnete Ärztin**
       I come as a friend   she is considered an excellent doctor

   iii) names of nationalities used after the verb 'to be':

       er ist Deutscher   **sie ist Französin von Geburt**
       he is a German   she is a Frenchwoman by birth

3. The indefinite article used as a pronoun

a) *special forms*

   When the indefinite article is used by itself, as a pronoun, it has the same forms as above, except that the masculine nominative is **einer** and the neuter nominative and accusative is **ein(e)s**.

b) *use*

   Used as a pronoun, it refers to some unspecified person or thing; it is often an alternative to **man**:

   was soll einer da machen?
   what should one do?

   ein(e)s von den Mädchen   **einer meiner Freunde**
   one of the girls   one of my friends

Note: the accusative and dative are used for the accusative and dative of **man**:

       man soll es offen sagen, wenn einem etwas nicht gefällt
       you should say so openly if you don't like something

       es kann einen schon ärgern, wenn man ...
       it can be very annoying if one ...

4. *irgendein*

   irgendein is usually translated by 'some ... or other'. It has the same endings as **ein** and can be used both as an article and as a pronoun:

   wir werden irgendeinen Film sehen
   we'll see some film or other

   irgendeiner hat's gesagt   **irgendeine Ausrede**
   someone or other said it   any old excuse

26 ARTICLES

For the plural, **irgendwelche** is used:

> **hat jemand irgendwelche Fragen?**
> has anyone any questions at all?

5. The indefinite article as adjective

ein can be used after the definite article, a demonstrative or possessive as an adjective. In such cases it has the appropriate adjective endings (see p 65-71):

> **der eine Besucher bleibt länger**
> one of the visitors is staying longer

> **die Frau des einen lebt noch**
> the wife of one of them is still alive

C. KEIN (no, not a, not any)

kein has the same endings as the indefinite article **ein,** but also has a plural form:

	MASCULINE	FEMININE	NEUTER	PLURAL ALL GENDERS
nom	**kein**	**keine**	**kein**	**keine**
acc	**keinen**	**keine**	**kein**	**keine**
gen	**keines**	**keiner**	**keines**	**keiner**
dat	**keinem**	**keiner**	**keinem**	**keinen**

a) It is used as a negative both for the indefinite article and for words without an article:

positive *negative*

ich habe Zeit **sie hat keine Zeit**
I have time she has no time

ich habe einen Computer **er hat keinen Computer**
I have a computer he hasn't got a computer

ich habe Ferien **er hat keine Ferien**
I'm on holiday he's not on holiday

It is always used when English has 'not a':

kein einziger Mensch kam
not a single person came

b) **kein** can also be used by itself, as a pronoun.

In that case, the masculine nominative singular is **keiner**, the neuter singular nominative and accusative is **kein(e)s**:

keiner weiß, wo er steckt
no-one knows where he is

D. DERJENIGE and DERSELBE (the one; the same)

These are declined in two parts, the **der** part having the forms of the definite article, the second part having regular endings for an adjective after the definite article (see p 65-6):

	MASCULINE	FEMININE	NEUTER	PLURAL ALL GENDERS
nom	derjenige	diejenige	dasjenige	diejenigen
acc	denjenigen	diejenige	dasjenige	diejenigen
gen	desjenigen	derjenigen	desjenigen	derjenigen
dat	demjenigen	derjenigen	demjenigen	denjenigen

derselbe follows the same pattern.

a) **derjenige** can be used before a noun or by itself, as a pronoun. It is used to specify someone or something about which more precise information is going to be given. Thus it is always followed either by a relative clause or by a noun in the genitive or by a preposition + noun.

A noun preceded by **derjenige** is always followed by a relative clause.

derjenige tends to be avoided, especially in colloquial German.

diejenigen, die schon Karten haben, sollen vortreten
those who already have tickets should come forward

diejenigen mit Karten sollen vortreten
those with tickets should come forward

kennst du diejenigen Mitglieder, die dagegen gestimmt haben?
do you know the members who voted against?

b) **derselbe** is used both before a noun and by itself, as a pronoun. It is the equivalent to the English 'the same', except that it is written as one word:

das ist nicht mehr dieselbe Mannschaft
they're not the same team any more

es läuft auf dasselbe hinaus
it amounts to the same thing

Note: the article (**der** *etc*) in **derselbe** can combine with some prepositions. It is then written as two words:

im selben Haus **zur selben Schule**
in the same house to the same school

ins selbe Theater
to the same theatre

c) ***dergleichen*** *('suchlike, of that kind')*

der gleiche is written as two words, except for **dergleichen** meaning 'suchlike'. **dergleichen** can be used before nouns or by itself, but in either case it does not change its form:

dergleichen Fälle **nichts dergleichen**
suchlike cases nothing of the sort

30 ARTICLES

E. DEMONSTRATIVES

dieser	jener	jeder	mancher	solcher	aller	welcher
this	that	each, every	some, many a	such	all	which

These are generally called demonstrative adjectives (or pronouns). Adjectives that follow them have the same endings as after the definite article.

1. Forms

	MASCULINE	FEMININE	NEUTER	PLURAL ALL GENDERS
nom	dieser	diese	dieses	diese
acc	diesen	diese	dieses	diese
gen	dieses	dieser	dieses	dieser
dat	diesem	dieser	diesem	diesen

The others have the same endings, except that **jeder** only occurs in the singular.

2. Use

a) *dieser* ('*this*')

Note: the neuter nominative and accusative is often shortened to **dies**.

dieser is used to point to a person or thing. It can be used before a noun or by itself, as a pronoun. It is very close to the English 'this':

> **gefällt dir dieser Mantel?**   **nein, ich nehme diesen**
> do you like this coat?   no, I'll take this one

It is often emphasised by the addition of **hier** or **da** after it or after the noun it goes with:

> **diese Jacke hier ist schöner**   **aber probier diese da an**
> this jacket here is nicer   but try on that one there

When standing alone before the verb **sein** (in all tenses) it is usually in the **dies** form, whatever the number or gender of the words it refers back to; the verb is singular or plural, according to the number of the noun following:

> **dies sind meine Eltern**   **dies hier ist meine Tochter**
> these are my parents   this is my daughter here

ARTICLES

dies(es) waren die besten Bilder
these were the best pictures

b) *jener ('that')*

jener is relatively little used in colloquial German. The word for 'that' as opposed to 'this' is usually **der/die/das** (see (c) below). In the following, somewhat formal, sentence, **jene** could be replaced by **die**, but is slightly more emphatic:

er zeigte jene Kraft, die ihm zu vielen Siegen verholfen hatte
he showed that strength which had brought him many victories

jener and **dieser** are used for 'the former' and 'the latter':

Männer und Frauen, diese Sorgen für andere, jene für sich
men and women, the former care for themselves, the latter for others

c) *der, die, das*

The definite article is also used in German to mean 'that'. Sometimes the word **da** is also added after the noun:

der Mann (da)   **die Schule (da)**
that man   that school

d) *jeder ('each, every')*

jeder can be used before the noun or by itself, as a pronoun:

jedes Kind weiß das   **jeder soll kommen**
every schoolboy knows that   everyone's to come

Note: **jedermann** is felt to be slightly stilted; **jeder** is the usual German for everyone.

jeder can be emphasised by the addition of **ein** before it; it still has the same endings:

ein jeder muß was mitbringen
everyone has to bring something

e) *mancher ('some, many a')*

mancher can be used before the noun or by itself, as a pronoun. It indicates an uncertain number and translation can range from 'a few' to 'some', even 'many':

manche älteren Leute   **manche hundert Mark**
some older people   a few hundred marks

ARTICLES

mancher Mann möchte reich sein
many a man would like to be rich

manches blieb unerledigt
quite a lot of things were unfinished

i) In the singular **manch** can be used without endings before an adjective + noun:

sie hat manch schöne Stadt gesehen
she has seen many a fair city

Note: this usage is highly literary.

ii) **manch** without endings can also be used before the indefinite article:

manch eine interessante Geschichte **manch ein Roman**
many an interesting story many a novel

Used without a noun the masculine nominative is **manch einer**:

manch einer erfährt das zu spät
many a man learns that too late

f) *solcher* ('such, such a')

i) In the singular **solcher** is rarely used with particular persons or objects. It is normally used with names of qualities, abstract nouns or substances.

solches Wetter! **magst du solchen Wein?**
such weather do you like such wine?

mit solcher Geschwindigkeit, daß ...
with such speed that ...

With particular persons or objects it is common to use **so ein**:

so ein Fahrer **haben Sie so eine Diskette?**
a driver like that do you have a diskette like this?

ii) In the plural it can be used with all nouns:

solche Frauen sind gefährlich
such women are dangerous

iii) It can also be used by itself, as a pronoun, usually in the plural:

ich kenne auch solche
I know people like that, too

In the singular it is only commonly used without a noun when it is neuter, in the form **solches**:

hast du je solches gehört?
have you ever heard anything like it?

iv) **solch** can be used without endings before an adjective + noun:

ein solch altes Schloß   **solch schicke Möbel**
such an old castle   such smart furniture

v) **solch** without endings can also be used with the indefinite article:

solch ein altes Schloß   **mit solch einem Freund**
such an old castle   with such a friend

Used without a noun the masculine nominative is **solch einer**, the neuter nominative and accusative **solch eines**:

solch einer war's   **hast du je solch einen gesehen?**
it was one like that   have you ever seen one like him?

vi) **solcher** can also be used after **ein** or **kein**. In that case it has the normal adjective endings (see p 67-8). *Compare:*

bei solchem schrecklichen Sturm
during such a terrible storm

with: **bei einem solchen schrecklichen Sturm**

g) **aller** (*'all, all the'*)

i) In the singular **aller** can only be used together with names for qualities, abstract nouns or substances:

bei aller Bewunderung   **er hat alles Geld ausgegeben**
in spite of all my admiration   he spent all the money

In the plural it can be used before any noun:

alle Spieler   **für alle Kunden**   **die beste von allen Gruppen**
all players   for all customers   the best of all groups

In the neuter singular and in the plural it can be used by itself, as a pronoun:

alles in Ordnung?   **nach allem, was du mir gesagt hast**
everything all right?   after all you've told me

Sie müssen alle kommen   **alle waren dagegen**
you must all come   everyone was against it

34 ARTICLES

Note: **alle Welt**   **die ganze Welt**
everybody   the whole world

Note: with most masculine and neuter nouns in the genitive singular the normal form is **allen**:

allen Ernstes
in all seriousness

ii) Before an article, demonstrative or possessive the normal form is **all**, without any ending; the article, demonstrative or possessive retains its normal endings.

Note that there is no German equivalent to 'of' in the English 'all of':

all unsere Bekannten
all of our acquaintances

mit all diesem Geld   **all die Männer**
with all this money   all of the men

As an alternative to **all das** and **all dies**, **das alles** and **dies alles** are possible.

Word order: after a pronoun:

es alles   **mit uns allen**   **für sie alle**
all of it   with all of us   for all of them

but: before **beide** or a number:

alle beide   **von allen vier(en)**
both of them   of all four of them

There are two possible orders for this; 'all three came' can be translated by:

alle drei sind gekommen
or: **sie sind alle drei gekommen**

h) ***welcher?*** *('which?')*

i) **welcher** is the interrogative article (sometimes called the interrogative adjective or pronoun). It can be used both before nouns and by itself, as a pronoun.

welche Farbe nehmen wir?
which colour shall we choose?

bei welcher Familie wohnt sie?
which family does she live with?

welches gefällt dir am besten?
which one do you like best?

welche kommen mit?
which ones of them are coming with us?

ii) Before the verb 'to be' (in any tense) the form **welches** is often used for all genders, singular and plural. The verb is singular or plural according to the number of the noun following:

welches ist der nächste Weg?
which is the shortest way?

welches (welche) waren die besten?
which were the best?

iii) **welch** may be used without endings before an adjective + noun to express an exclamation. This usage is rather literary, **was für ein** being generally preferred in colloquial German:

welch furchtbarer Kampf! **was für ein schlechtes Spiel!**
what a fearsome battle   what a poor game

iv) **welch** can be used with the indefinite article before a noun to express an exclamation:

welch ein schrecklicher Kerl!
what an awful fellow

v) **welcher** can also be used before a noun for exclamations; it is felt to be very stilted, although some standard phrases with feminine nouns are less so:

welche Freude!   **welche Ehre!**   **welche Schande!**
what joy   what an honour   what a disgrace

vi) As an interrogative, **welcher** can introduce a clause which is the object of a verb of telling, showing etc; the verb in the **welcher** clause then goes to the end. **welcher** can be used in this way either before a noun or alone:

sag mir, welche Kassette mehr kostet
tell me which cassette costs more

weißt du, welche mehr kostet?
do you know which one costs more?

vii) **welcher** can be used alone as an indefinite pronoun, replacing **etwas**, **einige** *etc*. In this usage it does not indicate a question. This is a very common colloquial usage:

ich hab kein Geld mehr. Hast du welches?
I've no money left. Have you any?

laß sie zu Hause — ich habe welche
leave them at home — I've got some

Note: the negative of **welcher** in this use is **kein**:

bring sie mit — ich hab keine
bring them with you — I haven't any

viii) **welcher** can be used as a relative pronoun without indicating a question. It is less common than **der/die/das** but is useful to avoid repetition:

das ist die Bluse, welche sie gewählt hat
that's the blouse she chose

wähle die, welche dir gefallen
choose those that you like

F. THE POSSESSIVE

1. Forms

There is a possessive form for each of the personal pronouns:

PRONOUN	POSSESSIVE
ich	mein
du	dein
er	sein
sie	ihr
es	sein
wir	unser
ihr	euer
Sie	Ihr
sie	ihr

They have the same endings as **ein** and **kein**, depending on the gender, number and case of the noun following:

	MASCULINE	FEMININE	NEUTER	PLURAL
nom	mein	meine	mein	meine
acc	meinen	meine	mein	meine
gen	meines	meiner	meines	meiner
dat	meinem	meiner	meinem	meinen

with the same endings for **dein**, **sein** *etc*

deine Tasche	**mit unserer Hilfe**	**für Ihre Kinder**
your bag	with our help	for your children

Notes on forms:

i) **euer** generally drops the **-e-** if it has an ending: **eure**, **euren** *etc*; **unser** often drops the **-e-** in spoken German, but it is normally kept when written.

ii) The possessives keep the same endings when they are preceded by **aller**, **dieser**, **jener**:

mit aller seiner Geschicklichkeit   **diese meine Freunde**
with all his skill   my friends here

but: **diese alten Freunde von mir**
these old friends of mine

iii) In letters **dein** and **euer** are written beginning with capitals:

ich habe Deinen Brief erhalten ...
I received your letter ...

38 ARTICLES

iv) For the replacement of the possessive by **dessen** or **deren**, see p 22-3.

2. Use

a) The possessive can also be used by itself, as a pronoun; in such cases the masculine nominative has the form **meiner**, **deiner**, **seiner** *etc*, and the neuter nominative and accusative have the form **meines**, **deines**, **seines** *etc*. Colloquially **meines** *etc* is often shortened to **meins** *etc*:

> **leih mir dein Rad, mein(e)s ist kaputt**
> lend me your bike, mine is broken
>
> **das ist ihr Platz, und das ist seiner**
> that's her place and that's his

b) As an adjectival noun the possessive has some idiomatic usages:

> **die Seinen**   **sie hat das Ihre getan**
> his family   she did her bit
>
> **grüß die Deinen**
> best wishes to your family

In sentences with noun + **sein** ('to be') + possessive, the possessives (except **Ihr/ihr**) often have no ending whatever the gender or number:

> **der Pulli ist mein**   **der Sieg war unser**
> that pullover is mine   victory was ours

c) The possessive can be used with the definite article as a pronoun (alternative to (a) above). In such cases it has the endings of an adjective after the definite article. This usage is generally regarded as literary:

> **dieser Bleistift ist der meine**
> this pencil is mine
>
> **du hast kein Auto? fahr mit dem meinen**
> you've no car? take mine

d) A further alternative is to use the form of the possessive plus **-ig** with the definite article: **der meinige**, **der deinige**, **der seinige**, **der ihrige**, **der unsrige**, **der eurige**, **der Ihrige**, **der ihrige**. This usage is also regarded as rather literary.

3. NOUNS

Nouns are naming words, which refer to persons, animals, things or abstract ideas. In German all nouns, not just proper names, are written beginning with a capital letter:

Haus **Ball**
house ball

A. GENDER

German nouns are either masculine, feminine or neuter in gender. The nouns themselves normally do not show this, but any preceding adjective or article 'agrees' with the noun by having the appropriate ending showing its gender plus number and case.

The gender should be learnt along with the noun, but often the meaning or ending will help you determine it, as set out in the guidelines below.

1. Masculine

a) *by meaning*

  i) names of male humans and animals:

der Sohn	**der Student**	**der Hahn**
son	student	cock

Note: the name for the species may be masculine, feminine or neuter:

der Elefant	**die Schlange**	**das Kamel**
elephant	snake	camel

  ii) names of days, months, seasons:

nächsten Mittwoch	**letzten Mai**	**der Herbst**
next Wednesday	last May	autumn

  iii) points of the compass, winds, etc:

der Süden	**der Monsun**	**der Hagel**
south	monsoon	hail

40 NOUNS

- iv) makes of cars:

    ein BMW **ein Opel** **ein Cadillac**

but: motor bicycles are feminine:

die BMW **die Harley-Davidson**

- v) names of rock and soil types:

der Quarz	**der Basalt**	**der Lehm**
quartz	basalt	clay

but: **die Kreide**
chalk

b) *by ending*

-en	**der Hafen** harbour	**der Wagen** car
-er	**der Arbeiter** worker	**der Kopfhörer** headphones
but:	**das Fenster** window	**das Messer** knife
	die Mutter mother	**die Tochter** daughter

and a few other neuter and feminine nouns

-ich	**der Teppich** carpet	**der Gänserich** gander
-ig	**der König** king	
-ing	**der Frühling** spring	**mein Liebling** my darling
-ismus	**der Terrorismus** terrorism	
-ist	**der Optimist** optimist	
-or	**der Horror** horror	**der Motor** motor
consonant + s	**der Schnaps** schnapps	**der Lachs** salmon

NOUNS   41

2. Feminine

a) *by meaning*

  i) names for female humans and animals:

die Mutter	**meine Frau**	**eine Kuh**
the mother	my wife	a cow

  ii) names for female occupations derived by adding **-in** to the masculine:

die Ärztin	**die Journalistin**	**die Geologin**
doctor	journalist	geologist

Note: names of chemicals ending in **-in** are neuter:

das Benzin
petrol

  iii) names of most common trees, fruits and flowers:

die Pappel	**die Kirsche**	**die Ananas**
poplar	cherry	pineapple
die Kiefer	**die Nelke**	**die Rose**
pine	carnation	rose

but:

der Ahorn	**der Apfel**	**der Pfirsich**
maple	apple	peach

  iv) makes of aeroplane and names of ships:

   die Boeing   **die Graf Spee**

but: **der Starfighter**   **der Airbus**

  v) numbers

   eine Null   **die Sieben**
   zero   (number) seven

b) *by ending*

   -a   **die Kamera**   **die Tuba**
          camera   tuba

   -ei   **die Kartei**
          card index

42 NOUNS

but:	not compounds of	**das Ei** egg	
	-enz	**die Frequenz** frequency	
	-heit	**die Freiheit** freedom	
	-ie	**die Chemie** chemistry	
but:		**das Genie** genius	
	-ik	**die Technik** technology	
but:		**der Atlantik** Atlantic	**der Pazifik** Pacific
		der Katholik Catholic	
	-keit	**die Süßigkeit** sweet	
	-schaft	**die Mannschaft** team	
	-ung	**die Eroberung** conquest	
but:		**der Schwung** verve	
	-tät	**die Pubertät** puberty	
	-tion	**die Reaktion** reaction	
	-ur	**die Natur** nature	

3. Neuter
a) *by meaning*
   i) names for the young of humans and animals:

das Kind	**das Baby**	**das Junge des Elefanten**
child	baby	the elephant calf

NOUNS

Note: **das Junge** is an adjectival noun, for endings see section 4 below.

das Kalb	**das Lamm**	**das Füllen**
calf	lamb	foal

ii) names of continents, towns and most countries:

das Europa der 20er Jahre
the Europe of the twenties

das Berlin meiner Kindheit
the Berlin of my childhood

das andere Deutschland
the other (part of) Germany

but: names of countries always preceded by the definite article are usually feminine:

die DDR	**die Türkei**
the GDR	Turkey

or plural: **die USA**
the USA

iii) nouns formed from other parts of speech, especially infinitives:

das Vergnügen	**sein Ja geben**	**das Hin und Her**
pleasure	to say yes	long deliberation

iv) diminutives with the endings **-chen**, **-lein**:

das Mädchen	**das Fräulein**	**das Städtchen**
girl	young woman	small town

v) fractions:

ein Sechstel
a sixth

vi) collectives beginning with the prefix **Ge-**:

das Gebirge	**das Gerede**	**das Geräusch**
the mountains	talk, gossip	noise

vii) most names for metals, chemical elements and medicaments:

das Messing	**das Uran**	**das Aspirin**
brass	uranium	aspirin

44 NOUNS

b) by ending

-ing (from English)	**das Hearing**	**das Meeting**	**das Petting**
-ma	**das Thema** subject	**das Dogma** dogma	
-ment	**das Regiment** regiment	**das Appartement** flat	

but:
           der Zement
           cement

      -tum   **das Eigentum**
                     property

but:
           der Irrtum   **der Reichtum**
           mistake   wealth

      -um   **das Zentrum**
                     centre

4. Adjectival nouns

All adjectives — and many past participles — can be made into nouns. They then begin with a capital letter but they keep the adjective endings:

    der Deutsche   *but*   **ein Deutscher**
    the German   a German

    viele Deutsche   *but*   **alle Deutschen**
    many Germans   all Germans

For the full list of endings see p 65-8.

a) *masculine and feminine*

Masculine and feminine nouns formed from adjectives generally refer to people:

    der Erste   **die Letzte**   **ein Neuer**
    the first one   the last one   a new one

Note: when an adjective refers back to a noun there is no capital letter, the noun previously mentioned being understood:

    der Deutsche hat gewonnen
    the German won

but: **zwei Läufer kommen, der deutsche führt knapp**
       two runners have appeared, the German has a short lead

NOUNS

b) *neuter*

Neuter nouns formed from adjectives most commonly refer to abstract ideas or qualities indicated by the adjective:

das Beste　　　　　　　**das Erschreckende**
the best　　　　　　　　　what is frightening

das eben Gesagte
what has just been said

i) Such nouns are often used with **an** + dative:

das Interessante an dieser Geschichte
what is interesting about this story

das Schlimmste an der Sache
the worst thing about it

ii) Such nouns are often used after **etwas, nichts, viel, wenig, alles**:

etwas Leckeres　　　**nichts Neues**　　　**alles Gute**
something tasty　　　　nothing new　　　　　all the best

Note: sometimes such words, when they are set phrases in common use, do not use the capital; if in doubt consult a dictionary:

im allgemeinen　　　**folgendes**　　　　**im großen und ganzen**
in general　　　　　　　the following　　　　by and large

c) *names of colours*

Names for colours are formed from the adjective but there are forms both with and without the adjective ending.

i) The form without the adjective ending is usually the name for the general colour:

das Blau des Himmels　　　**Rot steht dir nicht**
the blue of the sky　　　　　　red doesn't suit you

Grün ist meine Lieblingsfarbe
green is my favourite colour

ii) The form with the adjective ending usually refers to some specific item of that colour:

das Weiße seiner Augen　　　**das Gelbe vom Ei**
the whites of his eyes　　　　　the yellow of the egg

46 NOUNS

Note: for traffic lights the forms are **Rot** and **Grün**:

bei Rot soll man halten, bei Grün darf man fahren
you should stop on red, drive on at the green light

Note the plural for various shades of the same colour:

die verschiedenen Rottöne des Gemäldes
the different reds in the painting

5. Miscellaneous

a) The following words retain the same gender whatever sex of person they refer to:

der Mensch	human being
der Gast	guest
der Untertan	subject, vassal
die Geisel	hostage
die Person	person
die Wache	guard
die Waise	orphan
das Genie	genius
das Individuum	individual
das Staatsoberhaupt	head of state
das Opfer	victim
das Mitglied	member

b) Compound nouns have the gender of the final component:

die Urlaubsreise
holiday trip

c) For adjectival nouns see section 4 above.

d) Some nouns can have more than one gender:

der Joghurt	**das Joghurt**	**die Joghurt** (*colloquial*)
yoghurt	yoghurt	yoghurt

der Teil	**das Teil**
part	part, component

Note: compounds with **-teil** have only one gender:

der Vorteil	*but*	**das Gegenteil**
advantage		disadvantage

NOUNS 47

e) The following are the commonest nouns which change meaning according to gender.

Note: they usually have different plurals according to the gender.

	MASCULINE (der)	FEMININE (die)	NEUTER (das)
Band	book, volume	band (*music*)	tape, tie
Erbe	heir	–	inheritance
Gehalt	content	–	salary
Golf	bay	–	golf
Heide	heathen	heath	–
Hundert	–	100 (*number*)	100 (*amount*)
Hut	hat	protection	–
Junge	boy	–	young animal
Kiefer	jaw	pine tree	–
Kunde	customer	news	–
Laster	lorry	–	vice
Leiter	leader	ladder	–
Mangel	lack	mangle	–
Mark	–	Mark	marrow
Maß	–	beer measure	measurement
Mensch	human	–	tart (*insult*)
Moment	moment (*time*)	–	moment (*physics*)
Otter	otter	viper	–
Pack	stack	–	rabble
Schild	shield	–	sign
See	lake	sea	–
Steuer	–	tax	steering wheel
Stift	pin, pencil	–	foundation
Tau	dew	–	rope
Tausend	–	1000 (*number*)	1000 (*amount*)
Tor	fool	–	gate, goal
Verdienst	income	–	merit
Weise	wise man	manner, tune	–

48 NOUNS

B. THE FORMATION OF PLURALS

There are five main plural forms in German; three also sometimes have an umlaut on the stem vowel. These five forms are set out below with indications of the main types of nouns to which they apply. However, plural forms should be learnt together with the nouns.

1. No plural ending; some add an umlaut

Taken by   Masculine and neuter nouns ending in **-chen**, **-el**, **-en**, **-er**, **-lein**.

das Mädchen	die Mädchen	girl
der Hobel	die Hobel	plane (*carpentry*)
das Kabel	die Kabel	cable
der Braten	die Braten	roast
das Kissen	die Kissen	cushion
der Bagger	die Bagger	digger
das Messer	die Messer	knife
das Büchlein	die Büchlein	little book

Some masculine and occasional feminine and neuter nouns take an umlaut:

der Vogel	die Vögel	bird
der Laden	die Läden	shop
der Hammer	die Hämmer	hammer
das Kloster	die Klöster	monastery
die Mutter	die Mütter	mother
die Tochter	die Töchter	daughter

2. Plural ending -e

Taken by   Most masculine nouns, many neuter nouns, a group of common feminine nouns of one syllable and the few feminines ending in **-nis**; the s is doubled after **-nis** ending.

der Tag	die Tage	day
der Freund	die Freunde	friend
der Dom	die Dome	cathedral
der Monat	die Monate	month
der Bericht	die Berichte	report
das Haar	die Haare	hair
das Pfund	die Pfunde	pound
das Gesetz	die Gesetze	law

All feminine monosyllables, many masculine monosyllables and some masculine words formed with formed with prefix + monosyllable take an umlaut:

die Hand	die Hände	hand
die Kunst	die Künste	art
der Traum	die Träume	dream
der Knopf	die Knöpfe	button
der Einwand	die Einwände	objection
der Anfang	die Anfänge	beginning
das Ereignis	die Ereignisse	event
die Kenntnis	die Kenntnisse	knowledge

Note: **das Floß**   **die Flöße**   raft

3. Plural ending -(e)n

Note: the **e** is included after words ending in **-ei**, **-au**, and in consonants except for **-el**, **-er** endings; otherwise the ending is **-n**; the **n** is doubled after **-in** endings.

Taken by   A great many feminine nouns, a number of masculine nouns, and a small number of neuter monosyllables. None take an umlaut:

die Eitelkeit	die Eitelkeiten	vanity
die Hoffnung	die Hoffnungen	hope
die Ärztin	die Ärztinnen	doctor
die Bäckerei	die Bäckereien	bakery
die Au	die Auen	meadow
die Bahn	die Bahnen	railway
die Straße	die Straßen	street
die Schüssel	die Schüsseln	bowl
die Feder	die Federn	feather
der Mensch	die Menschen	human
der Nerv	die Nerven	nerve
das Bett	die Betten	bed

4. Plural ending -er

Taken by   A good number of neuter nouns, especially monosyllables, nouns ending in **-tum**, and a few masculine monosyllables. All take an umlaut if possible:

das Rad	die Räder	wheel
das Land	die Länder	country
das Lied	die Lieder	song

das Gespenst	die Gespenster	ghost
das Bistum	die Bistümer	bishopric
der Reichtum	die Reichtümer	wealth
der Strauch	die Sträucher	bush
der Geist	die Geister	spirit

5. Plural ending *-s*

Taken by Many foreign nouns, especially from English and French, nouns ending with a single vowel (except **-e**), abbreviations, proper names and a few technical terms to do with the weather and the sea. None take an umlaut:

das Team	die Teams	team
die City	die Citys	city centre
das Brikett	die Briketts	coal briquette
das Sofa	die Sofas	sofa
der Uhu	die Uhus	owl
ein Sozi	die Sozis	socialist
der Pulli	die Pullis	pullover
der LKW	die LKWs	lorry
Frau Müller	die Müllers	the Müllers
das Tief	die Tiefs	depression
das Deck	die Decks	deck

6. Double plurals

Some nouns have two plural forms with difference of meaning; those given below are the commonest:

die Bank	die Bänke	bench
	die Banken	bank
der Bau	die Baue	animal's lair
	die Bauten	building
die Mutter	die Mütter	mother
	die Muttern	nut (*for bolt*)
der Strauß	die Strauße	ostrich
	die Sträuße	bouquet
das Wort	die Wörter	single words
	die Worte	words (*combined in a sentence*)

Note: The nouns with double gender listed on p 47 above will also have a different plural form for each gender.

NOUNS 51

7. Singular or plural?

Whilst almost all nouns have both singular and plural forms, some occur only in the singular and a few only in the plural. Usage here is not always the same as in English; consult a dictionary if in doubt.

a) *nouns only occurring in the singular*

  i) names of substances:

das Fleisch	**das Gummi**	**die Milch**
meat	rubber	milk
die Butter	**das Leder**	**der Schnee**
butter	leather	snow

Note: these often form plurals by being compounded with either **-sorten** or **-arten**:

verschiedene Buttersorten   **zwei Getreidearten**
different types of butter   two kinds of grain

Note: singular is sometimes used for plural:

zwei Bier, bitte
two beers, please

  ii) many collectives:

das Vieh	**die Bourgeoisie**	**die Polizei**
cattle	the bourgeoisie	the police
das Gepäck	**der Schmuck**	**das Publikum**
luggage	jewellery	the audience

  iii) many abstract nouns. But note that some can also be used in a specific as well as a general sense and then have a plural, eg **der Spaß** = enjoyment has no plural but **der Spaß** = joke has the plural **die Späße**.

der Fleiß	**die Hitze**	**der Aufbau**
diligence	heat	building up

Note: abstracts often have parallel forms which can be put into the plural, eg **der Rat** (advice) has no plural but **der Ratschlag** (piece of advice) has the plural **die Ratschläge**.

  iv) names of colours:

das Schwarz	**das Grün**	**das Blau**
black	green	blue

52 NOUNS

Note: names for colours formed, as the first two above, from the adjective with no ending can be used in the singular with plural meaning eg **die zwei Grün** ('the two greens') (see also section A4c).

v) nouns formed from adjectives (see section 4 above) when they do not refer to people and nouns formed from infinitives when they refer to an activity and not to an object:

das Beste ('the best thing') has no plural but **die Beste** ('the best woman') has the plural **die Besten**.

das Schreiben ('the act of writing') has no plural but **das Schreiben** ('the letter') has the plural **die Schreiben**.

b) *nouns only occurring in the plural*

i) some geographical names:

die Niederlande
the Netherlands

ii) a few nouns of a collective nature:

die Eltern	**die Leute**	**die Ferien**
parents	people	holidays
die Kosten	**die Antiquitäten**	**die Möbel**
costs	antiques	furniture

Note: modern German sometimes uses the awkward singular

der Elternteil
parent

NOUNS

C. CASES

There are four cases in German: nominative, accusative, genitive and dative. They are indicated by systems of endings (called declensions) on any articles or adjectives preceding the noun. There are also a few endings on nouns, as set out below.

The purpose of the cases is to indicate the relationship between nouns and other elements of the sentence or, alternatively, a noun's function in the sentence.

1. The nominative

a) *as the subject of verbs:*

    der Mittelstürmer schießt
    the centre forward shoots

b) *after the verbs **sein, werden, bleiben, heißen, sich betrachten als, sich nennen**, and some other similar verbs where the noun complement to the verb is regarded as being in apposition to the subject:*

    er nennt sich mein Freund
    he calls himself *my friend*

2. The accusative

a) *as the object of verbs:*

    der Stürmer schießt ein Tor
    the forward shoots *a goal*

b) *after certain prepositions:* (see p 194-206)

c) *in certain adverbial phrases, especially of time:*

    er sitzt den ganzen Tag herum
    he just sits around *all day*

d) *the so-called absolute accusative (literary usage):*

    den Mantel um die Schultern, ging er hinaus
    his coat over his shoulders, he went out

3. The genitive

a) *to express possession and similar relationships between two nouns:*

> **das Zimmer *seines Chefs***
> his boss's office
>
> **die Reparatur *des Wagens***
> the repair *of the car*

Note: this is very often used in contexts where the English genitive is also used.

b) *in certain adverbial phrases:*

> **eines Tages**   **meines Erachtens**
> one day   in my opinion

c) *after certain prepositions:* (see p 207-9)

d) *when dependent on certain adjectives:*

> **er ist sich *seiner Verantwortung* bewußt**
> he is aware *of his responsibility*

4. The dative

a) *as the indirect object:*

> **er versprach *seiner Frau* die Treue**
> he promised to be faithful *to his wife*

Note that by no means all German verbs that 'take the dative' are obvious from their English equivalents:

> **er folgte *dem Verbrecher***
> he followed *the criminal*

b) *after certain prepositions:* (see p 189-93, 209)

c) *when dependent on certain adjectives:*

> **sie ist *ihrer Mutter* sehr ähnlich**
> she is very like *her mother*

NOUNS 55

D. THE DECLENSION OF NOUNS

All masculine and neuter nouns end in **-(e)s** in the genitive singular.

Some masculine and neuter nouns, mostly monosyllables, can take an **-e** ending in the dative plural. This is optional and is normally used for reasons of rhythm. There are a few idiomatic expressions where it is required, eg **im Grunde** ('basically'), but in almost all cases it is not wrong to omit it, eg **zu Haus** *or* **zu Hause** ('at home').

All nouns end in **-n** in the dative plural, except those forming the plural with **-s**. Nouns that do not have **-n** in the plural ending add **-(e)n**.

1. Masculine

	SINGULAR	PLURAL	
nom	der Vater	die Väter	father
acc	den Vater	die Väter	
gen	des Vaters	der Väter	
dat	dem Vater	den Vätern	

	SINGULAR	PLURAL	
nom	der Tag	die Tage	day
acc	den Tag	die Tage	
gen	des Tag(e)s	der Tage	
dat	dem Tag(e)	den Tagen	

a) A group of masculine nouns, often called weak nouns, takes the ending **-(e)n** in all cases apart from the nominative singular:

	SINGULAR	PLURAL	
nom	der Löwe	die Löwen	lion
acc	den Löwen	die Löwen	
gen	des Löwen	der Löwen	
dat	dem Löwen	den Löwen	

	SINGULAR	PLURAL	
nom	der Christ	die Christen	Christian
acc	den Christen	die Christen	
gen	des Christen	der Christen	
dat	dem Christen	den Christen	

	SINGULAR	PLURAL	
nom	der Student	die Studenten	student
acc	den Studenten	die Studenten	
gen	des Studenten	der Studenten	
dat	dem Studenten	den Studenten	

nom	**der Herr**	**die Herren**	gentleman
acc	**den Herrn**	**die Herren**	
gen	**des Herr(e)n**	**der Herren**	
dat	**dem Herrn**	**den Herren**	

Masculine nouns which have **-(e)n** endings in the singular consist of:

  i) nouns ending in **-e** denoting humans or animals:

der Erbe
heir

der Zeuge
witness

der Bulgare
Bulgarian

der Biologe
biologist

  ii) a number of monosyllables ending with a consonant and denoting humans or animals:

der Bär
bear

der Fürst
prince

der Held
hero

der Mensch
human

der Narr
fool

der Prinz
prince

der Zar
Tsar

plus **der Bauer**
farmer

der Nachbar
neighbour

  iii) words derived from foreign words with endings such as **-ant**, **-ent**, **-graph**, **-ist** and others; most, but not all, are names for human occupations:

der Emigrant
emigré

der Polizist
policeman

der Bürokrat
bureaucrat

der Astronom
astronomer

der Automat
automat

der Athlet
athlete

der Doktorand
PhD candidate

der Fotograf
photographer

der Pilot
pilot

der Bandit
bandit

NOUNS

b) A small number of masculine nouns have **-(e)n** in the plural and in the accusative and dative singular but form the genitive singular by adding **-(e)ns**; **das Herz** is similar except for the accusative singular:

	SINGULAR	PLURAL	
nom	**der Name**	**die Namen**	name
acc	**den Namen**	**die Namen**	
gen	**des Namens**	**der Namen**	
dat	**dem Namen**	**den Namen**	
nom	**das Herz**	**die Herzen**	heart
acc	**das Herz**	**die Herzen**	
gen	**des Herzens**	**der Herzen**	
dat	**dem Herzen**	**den Herzen**	

Similar to this is: **der Buchstabe** letter

c) *There is a small group of words with a double form in the nominative which take* **-ns** *in the genitive singular whichever nominative form is used:*

der Friede/Frieden peace	**der Funke/Funken** spark
der Gedanke/Gedanken thought	**der Glaube/Glauben** belief
der Same/Samen seed	**der Wille/Willen** will

	SINGULAR	PLURAL	
nom	**der Funke(n)**	**die Funken**	spark
acc	**den Funken**	**die Funken**	
gen	**des Funkens**	**der Funken**	
dat	**dem Funken**	**den Funken**	

2. Feminine

	SINGULAR	PLURAL	
nom	**die Frau**	**die Frauen**	woman
acc	**die Frau**	**die Frauen**	
gen	**der Frau**	**der Frauen**	
dat	**der Frau**	**den Frauen**	
nom	**die Nacht**	**die Nächte**	night
acc	**die Nacht**	**die Nächte**	
gen	**der Nacht**	**der Nächte**	
dat	**der Nacht**	**den Nächten**	

3. Neuter

	SINGULAR	PLURAL	
nom	das Gebäude	die Gebäude	building
acc	das Gebäude	die Gebäude	
gen	des Gebäudes	der Gebäude	
dat	dem Gebäude	den Gebäuden	
nom	das Gras	die Gräser	grass
acc	das Gras	die Gräser	
gen	des Grases	der Gräser	
dat	dem Gras(e)	den Gräsern	

4. Miscellaneous notes on forms

a) *-s* or *-es* in genitive?

i) **-es** is always added after words ending in **-s, -ß, -x, -z, -sch**:

der Krebs > **des Krebses**　　**der Sitz** > **des Sitzes**
crab　　　　　　　　　　　　seat

der Kitsch > **des Kitsches**
kitsch

ii) **-es** is often added after a word which ends with a double consonant:

der Kopf > **des Kopfes**　　**das Hemd** > **des Hemdes**
head　　　　　　　　　　　　shirt

iii) **-es** is always added to　　**Gott** > **Gottes**
　　　　　　　　　　　　　　　God

iv) **-s** is normally added to words ending with an unstressed syllable:

der Anfang > **des Anfangs**
beginning

v) **-s** is normally added to words ending with a vowel or vowel + **h**:

das Kino > **des Kinos**　　**der Schuh** > **des Schuhs**
cinema　　　　　　　　　　　shoe

vi) **-s** is added to most foreign nouns and to nouns of colour:

das Restaurant > des Restaurants
restaurant

das Rot > des Rots
red

vii) foreign words ending in **-as**, **-os**, **-us** have no extra ending in the genitive singular:

der Mythos > des Mythos
myth

der Kommunismus > des Kommunismus
communism

b) Neuter nouns ending in **-nis** double the **-s** before the genitive ending:

das Bildnis > des Bildnisses
portrait

5. The Saxon Genitive

The so-called Saxon genitive in which the genitive word comes first is used for proper names (see section 6 below), eg **Bachs Kantaten**. Otherwise it is uncommon but is sometimes used in literary style:

des Tages Hitze
the heat of the day

6. The genitive of proper names and titles

a) All names take an **-s** ending in the genitive, whether masculine or feminine:

Pauls Vater   **Monikas Freund**
Paul's father   Monika's friend

Frau Schmidts Geburtstag
Mrs Schmidt's birthday

i) Names consisting of more than one element take the **-s** on the last part:

die Stücke Friedrich Dürrenmatts
Friedrich Dürrenmatt's plays

60 NOUNS

Exceptions are some medieval names:

die Werke Gottfrieds von Straßburg
Gottfried von Straßburg's works

ii) Names ending in **s**, **ß**, **x**, **z** cannot be dealt with in this way. The addition of **-ens** (eg **Fritzens**) was common but is now felt to be old-fashioned. The addition of an apostrophe after the **-s** is still sometimes used in written German (eg **Grass' Stücke** - 'Grass's plays'), but in general the problem is avoided by using **von** or **des**:

der Einfluß von Marx   **die Reise des Kolumbus**
Marx's influence   Columbus' journey

iii) The genitive **-s** is omitted when the proper name is preceded by an article in the genitive:

die Zeugnisse der Luise
Luise's reports

b) When a name is preceded by a title, only the name takes the **-s**:

die Politik Präsident Reagans
President Reagan's policies

Tante Friedas Schmuck
aunt Frieda's jewellery

but: **Herr** is always declined (in the accusative and dative as well):

Herrn Köpkes Angebot
Mr Köpke's offer

Herrn Professor Winters Aufsatz
Professor Winter's essay

ein Brief an Herrn Doktor Weiß
a letter to Doctor Weiß

Note: letters should be addressed to **Herrn X**; the word **an** is often put before, but is anyway always understood.

c) After **statt**, **trotz**, **wegen** neither title nor name is declined:

trotz Peter   **wegen Direktor Braun**
in spite of Peter   because of Director Braun

d) When preceded by an article, demonstrative or possessive neither title nor name is now generally declined:

>   **das Schwert des General Herder**
>   General Herder's sword

e) Additional titles coming after the name are always declined:

>   **die Abdankung Eduards des Siebenten**
>   the abdication of Edward VII
>
>   **das Leben Peters des Großen**
>   the life of Peter the Great

4. ADJECTIVES

Adjectives are describing words which usually accompany a noun (or a pronoun) and tell us what someone or something is like:

ein kleines Dorf
a little village

die neue Platte
the new record

meine Jacke ist rot
my jacket is red

es war fantastisch
it was fantastic

A. AGREEMENT

1. Use

There is a major difference between English and German in the predicative use of adjectives (eg after is, are, were) and their attributive use (before nouns and pronouns). In the sentences

PREDICATIVE   ATTRIBUTIVE
my car is old   *and*   I drive an old car

the word 'old' appears twice, in identical form. But in the German sentences

mein Wagen ist alt *and* **ich fahre einen alten Wagen**
my car is old   I drive an old car

the word **alt** appears once with and once without an ending.

The predicative use is so similar to English that it should not be a problem. However, German adjectives used attributively can prove troublesome, since only one of a number of endings is ever correct in a given context. The rules governing these endings are set out below, but first here are some more examples to illustrate this important difference:

PREDICATIVE   ATTRIBUTIVE

das Boot ist neu   **ich brauche ein neues Boot**
the boat is new   I need a new boat

seine Eltern waren reich   **er kam mit seinen reichen Eltern nicht aus**
his parents were rich   he couldn't get on with his rich parents

ADJECTIVES

2. Endings

The endings of an attributive adjective in German are determined by the noun which follows it, according to three factors:

- **a)** *its gender* (whether masculine, feminine or neuter)
- **b)** *its number* (is it singular or plural?)
- **c)** *its case* (nominative, accusative *etc*).

In addition, there are variations, depending on whether the adjective comes after

- a) a definite article (**der, die, das** *etc*)
- b) an indefinite article (**ein, eine** *etc*)
- *or* c) is not preceded by any article, pronoun or possessive adjective.

3. Participles as adjectives

a) Present participles may be used as attributive adjectives:

ein weinendes Baby   **bellende Hunde**
a crying baby   barking dogs

They can also be used in adjectival phrases:

das gerade vorbeifahrende Auto
the car that's overtaking now

b) Past participles of transitive verbs may be used both attributively (as an adjective and in a phrase) and predicatively:

die verlorene Stadt   **das Geschirr ist abgewaschen**
the lost city   the dishes are washed

wegen des noch tiefer gesunkenen Dollars
because of the dollar that has fallen even lower

4. Exceptions

Exceptionally, the form of certain adjectives does not change, no matter what precedes them or what the gender, number or case of the following noun. These exceptions are:

a) *the adjective form of town names*

wer liest die Londoner Times?
who reads the London Times?

wir treffen uns in einem Glasgower Lokal
we'll meet in a Glasgow pub

64 ADJECTIVES

b) *halb* and *ganz* with towns, countries and continents

    in ganz Hamburg   **ganz Schottland**
    throughout Hamburg   the whole of Scotland

but: **die ganze Schweiz**
      the whole of Switzerland

(For the use of the article, see p. 43)

c) *rosa*, *lila* and *prima*

    ein rosa/lila Kleid   **eine prima Idee**
    a pink/lilac dress   a great idea

Note: adjectives ending in **-el** and **-er** drop the **e** before the **l** or **r** when they are used attributively:

dunkel	>	**ein dunkler Anzug**
dark		a dark suit
teuer	>	**eine teure Kamera**
expensive		an expensive camera

5. Adjectives relating to countries

Adjectives formed from the names of countries or continents are written with an initial lower case letter, not a capital:

    italienisches Eis   **die französische Hauptstadt**
    Italian ice-cream   the French capital

ADJECTIVES 65

B. ADJECTIVE ENDINGS

1. After the definite article (der, die, das)

	MASCULINE	FEMININE	NEUTER	PLURAL ALL GENDERS
nom	-e	-e	-e	-en
acc	-en	-e	-e	-en
gen	-en	-en	-en	-en
dat	-en	-en	-en	-en

Examples:

a) *nominative*

Masc Sing
der alte Mann wohnt hier
the old man lives here

Fem Sing
die neue Rektorin heißt Ulrike
the new headmistress is called Ulrike

Neut Sing
das grüne Kleid ist besonders schick
the green dress is extremely chic

Plural
die blauen Fahrräder kosten mehr
the blue bicycles cost more

b) *accusative*

Masc Sing
haben Sie den alten Mann gesehen?
have you seen the old man?

Fem Sing
ich kenne die neue Rektorin schon
I already know the new headmistress

Neut Sing
niemand hat das grüne Kleid gekauft
no-one has bought the green dress

Plural
wo kann man die blauen Fahrräder bekommen?
where can one get the blue bicycles?

ADJECTIVES

c) *genitive*

> *Masc Sing*
> **das sind die Kinder des alten Mannes**
> those are the old man's children
>
> *Fem Sing*
> **das Büro der neuen Rektorin ist rechts**
> the new headmistress's office is on the right
>
> *Neut Sing*
> **der Preis des grünen Kleid(e)s ist zu hoch**
> the price of the green dress is too high
>
> *Plural*
> **kennen Sie den Hersteller der blauen Fahrräder?**
> do you know who manufactures the blue bicycles?

d) *dative*

> *Masc Sing*
> **die Nachbarn helfen dem alten Mann**
> the neighbours help the old man
>
> *Fem Sing*
> **wir verstehen uns gut mit der neuen Rektorin**
> we get on well with the new headmistress
>
> *Neut Sing*
> **im grünen Kleid sehen Sie gut aus**
> you look good in the green dress
>
> *Plural*
> **mit den blauen Fahrrädern habe ich viel Erfolg**
> I'm having a lot of success with the blue bicycles

Note: adjectives used after the following words take the same endings as for the definite article:

der/die/dasjenige	the
der/die/dasselbe	the same
dieser, diese, dieses	this
irgendwelcher	some (or other)
jeder, jede, jedes	each
jener, jene, jenes	that
mancher, manche, manches	many a
solcher, solche, solches	such
welcher? welche? welches?	which?
alle *(pl)*	all
beide *(pl)*	both

ADJECTIVES 67

2. After the indefinite article

	MASCULINE	FEMININE	NEUTER
nom	-er	-e	-es
acc	-en	-e	-es
gen	-en	-en	-en
dat	-en	-en	-en

Examples:

a) *nominative*

> *Masc Sing*
> **ein deutscher Film läuft heute im Kino**
> there's a German film on today in the cinema
>
> *Fem Sing*
> **eine kleine Stadt liegt nicht weit von hier**
> there's a little town not far from here
>
> *Neut Sing*
> **ein weißes Kaninchen wäre ein schönes Geschenk!**
> a white rabbit would be a lovely present!

b) *accusative*

> *Masc Sing*
> **einen deutschen Film sieht man nicht oft**
> you don't often get the chance to see a German film
>
> *Fem Sing*
> **das braucht eine halbe Stunde**
> that will take half an hour
>
> *Neut Sing*
> **hast du ein tragbares Radio?**
> have you got a portable radio?

c) *genitive*

> *Masc Sing*
> **der Titel eines deutschen Film(e)s**
> the title of a German film
>
> *Fem Sing*
> **im Laufe einer schlaflosen Nacht**
> in the course of a sleepless night
>
> *Neut Sing*
> **das Foto eines alten Pferd(e)s**
> the photo of an old horse

68 ADJECTIVES

d) *dative*

Masc Sing
man unterhielt die Besucher mit einem deutschen Film
the visitors were entertained with a German film

Fem Sing
nach einer langen Pause
after a long pause

Neut Sing
außer einem langweiligen Fußballspiel war nichts los
apart from a boring game of football there was nothing happening

Note:

i) in addition, adjectives used after the following words take the same endings as above, when used in the singular:

irgendein/eine/ein   **kein, keine, kein**
some (or other)   no

all possessive adjectives, eg **mein** (my), **Ihr** (your)

ii) after **keine** and possessive adjectives in the plural, all adjectives end in **-en**, whatever case they are used in (see section B1).

3. Without any preceding article

	MASCULINE	FEMININE	NEUTER	PLURAL ALL GENDERS
nom	-er	-e	-es	-e
acc	-en	-e	-es	-e
gen	-en	-er	-en	-er
dat	-em	-er	-em	-en

Examples:

a) *nominative*

Masc Sing
feiner Wein kostet viel
good wine costs a lot

Fem Sing
englische Studentin sucht Arbeit
female English student seeks work

Neut Sing
eiskaltes Wasser schmeckt gut
ice-cold water tastes good

Plural
junge Leute sind besonders willkommen
young people are especially welcome

b) *accusative*

Masc Sing
er hat furchtbaren Hunger
he is incredibly hungry

Fem Sing
Polizei fängt wilde Katze
Police catch wild cat

Neut Sing
ich trinke gern eiskaltes Wasser
I like drinking ice-cold water

Plural
sie hat wunderbare Augen
she's got wonderful eyes

c) *genitive*

Masc Sing
ein Glas guten Wein(e)s genügt (*more usual*: **guter Wein**)
one glass of good wine is sufficient

Fem Sing
französischer Herkunft
of French extraction

Neut Sing
der Geschmack selbstgebackenen Brot(e)s
the taste of home-made bread

Plural
der Genuß alkoholischer Getränke
the consumption of alcoholic drinks

d) *dative*

Masc Sing
mit großem Erfolg
with great success

ADJECTIVES

Fem Sing
aus guter Familie
from a good home

Neut Sing
unter lautem Stöhnen
amid loud groans

Plural
im Vergleich zu japanischen Managern
in comparison with Japanese managers

Note:

i) In addition, adjectives used after the following words take the same endings as above:

★ *singular only*

ein bißchen	**ein wenig**	**solch**
a little	a little	such
viel	**wenig**	**welch**
much	little	what!

solch würzigen Käse habe ich noch nie gegessen!
I've never eaten such strong cheese!

unter viel verdientem Beifall verließ sie die Bühne
to much deserved applause she left the stage

★ *singular and plural*

mehr	**weniger**	**was für**
more	less, fewer	what (kind of)

mit mehr finanzieller Unterstützung
with more financial support

mit weniger regionalen Zeitungen
with fewer regional newspapers

★ *plural only*

einige	**ein paar**	**einzelne**
some	some, a few	individual
mehrere	**viele**	**wenige**
several	many	few

★ *numbers* (**zwei**, **drei**, **vier** *etc*)

es gibt nur noch ein paar schwierige Fälle
there are just a few difficult cases left

trotz mehrerer strenger Warnungen
despite several stern warnings

gegen den Rat zweier meiner Freunde
against the advice of two of my friends

ii) After **etwas**, **mehr**, **nichts**, **viel** and **wenig**, but when used without a following noun, adjectives are written with an initial capital letter and take the same endings as a neuter noun (see p 45):

nichts Besonderes ist heute passiert
nothing in particular happened today

wer hat (et)was Interessantes zu berichten?
who has something interesting to report?

er hat in seinem Leben nur wenig Gutes getan
he hasn't done much good in his life

iii) If two adjectives come together before a noun, both take the same endings:

die Blätter des großen alten Baumes
the leaves of the big old tree

ein Kind mit gutem artigem Benehmen
a well-behaved child

ADJECTIVES

C. COMPARATIVES AND SUPERLATIVES

People or things can be compared to others by using:

> **so** + adjective + **wie**
> as + adjective + as

or **ebenso/genauso/geradeso** + adjective + **wie**
just as + adjective + as

> **er ist (eben)so groß wie ich**
> he is (just) as tall as me/I am

However, when the comparison involves superiority the comparative and superlative forms of the adjective are used.

Like English, German adjectives form the comparative by adding **-er** and the superlative by adding **-st** or **-est**:

klein	**kleiner**	**(der) kleinst(e)**
small	smaller	smallest

Note: this scheme is applied more consistently in German than in English:

intelligent	**intelligenter**	**(der) intelligentest(e)**
intelligent	more intelligent	most intelligent

1. Comparative adjectives

a) *formation*

  i) As with adjectives in their basic form, comparative adjectives only take an ending (to indicate gender, number and case) when used attributively. These endings (see section B) are added to the standard **-er** of the comparative:

  die Farbe muß heller sein
  the colour must be lighter

but: **wir möchten eine hellere Farbe**
we'd like a lighter colour

  dieses Nilpferd ist so dick!
  this hippo is so fat!

but: **ein noch dickeres Nilpferd**
an even fatter hippo

ADJECTIVES

Note: Adjectives ending in **-el** and **-er** normally drop the **e** before the **l** or **r** when they are used in the comparative:

dieses Zimmer da ist dunkel   **aber dieses hier ist dunkler**
that room is dark   but this one is darker

ii) Some common one-syllable adjectives add an umlaut (and **-er**) in the comparative. The most common are:

alt	(old)	> **älter**	(older, elder)
arm	(poor)	> **ärmer**	(poorer)
dumm	(stupid)	> **dümmer**	(more stupid)
groß	(big, great)	> **größer**	(bigger, greater)
hart	(hard)	> **härter**	(harder)
jung	(young)	> **jünger**	(younger)
kalt	(cold)	> **kälter**	(colder)
klug	(intelligent)	> **klüger**	(more intelligent)
kurz	(short)	> **kürzer**	(shorter)
lang	(long)	> **länger**	(longer)
schwach	(weak)	> **schwächer**	(weaker)
stark	(strong)	> **stärker**	(stronger)
warm	(warm)	> **wärmer**	(warmer)

ich brauche einen jüngeren Mann!
I need a younger man/husband!

mein Bericht war lang, aber deiner war bestimmt länger
my report was long, but yours was definitely longer

iii) Note the comparative forms of the following:

gut	(good)	> **besser**	(better)
hoch	(high, tall)	> **höher**	(higher, taller)
viel	(much, a lot of)	> **mehr**	(more)

b) *usage*

i) In addition to the attributive use of comparatives:

ich kenne einen kürzeren Weg
I know a shorter way

and the simple predicative use:

Big Ben ist höher
Big Ben is taller

an explicit comparison between two people or things can be made by adding **als**:

sie bekommt ein höheres Stipendium als ich
she gets a bigger grant than me/than I do

74 ADJECTIVES

ihre Bibliothek ist älter als unsere
their library is older than ours

ii) Note, however, the set expression **denn je**:

besser denn je **weißer denn je**
better than ever whiter than ever

iii) Note, also, the construction **je** + comparative, **desto/um so** + comparative:

je eher, desto besser.
the sooner, the better.

je kleiner der Preis (ist), um so größer (ist) die Wirkung
the lower the price (is), the greater the effect

iv) A small number of adjectives can be used in the comparative form without any obvious sense of comparison:

eine ältere Dame **auf längere Zeit**
an elderly lady for a while

2. Superlative adjectives

a) *formation*

i) The German superlative adjective is formed by combining the definite article (**der/die/das**) with an adjective plus suffix **-(e)st** and ending.

ii) Superlatives take endings when used both attributively and predicatively. (Compare the basic form of adjectives and comparatives, which only take an ending when used attributively.)

iii) When used attributively, these endings, which are added to the **-(e)st** suffix, are the same as those in section B1:

die berühmteste Philosophin ihrer Generation
the most famous woman philosopher of her generation

mit dem kostbarsten Ring der Welt
with the most expensive ring in the world

Note: the **e** in adjectives ending in **-el** and **-er** is retained in the superlative:

das dunkelste Zimmer von allen
the darkest room of all

ADJECTIVES

iv) The common one-syllable adjectives that add an umlaut in the comparative (see section C1) do the same in the superlative.

der älteste Präsident der USA
the oldest President of the USA

v) Note the following irregular forms of the superlative:

gut	(good)	>	**(der) best-** *etc*	(best)
hoch	(high, tall)	>	**(der) höchst-** *etc*	(highest, tallest)
nah	(near)	>	**(der) nächst-** *etc*	(nearest, next)
viel	(much, a lot of)	>	**(der) meist-** *etc*	(most)

vi) Another form of the superlative adjective comes from combining **am** and an adjective plus **-(e)sten**:

| **billig** | (cheap) | > **am billigsten** | ([the] cheapest) |

This construction can only be used predicatively or after the verb:

dieser hier ist am billigsten
this one here is the cheapest

Note that it does not have any endings.

b) *usage*

i) Superlative expressions are often not complete without mention of the people or things which act as a reference group:

das schlechteste Wetter des Sommers
the worst weather of the summer

wer ist die mutigste von euch?
who's the bravest of you (girls)?

The words 'des Sommers' or 'von euch' are the reference groups.

ii) If a reference group is mentioned, the form of the superlative adjective with the definite article is the most usual.

iii) If no reference group is mentioned, both the form with the definite article and that with **am** can be used:

diese Eier sind die billigsten/am billigsten
these eggs are (the) cheapest

Note: with **best**, only one form is possible:

er ist einfach der beste
he's simply the best

ADJECTIVES

iv) A small number of adjectives can be used in the superlative form without any obvious sense of comparison:

es ist höchste Zeit **im äußersten Fall kostet es 2 Mark**
it's high time it'll cost 2 marks at the outside

v) To express 'in' as in phrases like 'the biggest in the world' *etc*, German uses either **in** or the genitive case:

die größte Stadt Deutschlands/in Deutschland
the biggest town in Germany

vi) Note also the following constructions with superlatives:

der meistgesungene Schlager
the most (frequently) sung hit

der meistgenannte Autor
the author mentioned most often

as well as the set expression **bestgehaßt** as in:

der bestgehaßte Politiker
the most hated politician

5. ADVERBS

There are two main differences between German and English adverbs:

(a) many German adverbs have the same form as the corresponding adjective:

die Wohnung ist billig *(adj)* **er lebt billig** *(adv)*
the flat is cheap   he lives cheaply

(b) the word order with adverbs often differs from English:

sie übt oft Klavier
she often practises the piano

er fährt morgen nach Hause
he's going home tomorrow

A. FORMATION

1. Words which are exclusively adverbs

da (there)   **sehr** (very)   **geradeaus** (straight on)

da sind sie!   **sehr nett**   **nur geradeaus!**
there they are!   very nice   keep straight on!

2. Adverbs identical in form with adjectives

ADJECTIVE   ADVERB
schön (beautiful) **schön** (beautifully)
furchtbar (terrible) **furchtbar** (terribly)

sie ist schön, und sie singt auch schön
she's beautiful, and she sings beautifully too

er hat furchtbar gespielt — es war wirklich furchtbar, nicht?
he played terribly — it was really terrible, wasn't it?

3. Adverbs formed from participles

sie spricht zögernd   **übertrieben groß**
she speaks hesitantly   exaggeratedly large

4. Adverbs formed from other parts of speech plus suffix

a) *-lich*

ADJECTIVE	ADVERB
neu (new, recent)	**neulich** (recently)
kurz (short)	**kürzlich** (recently)

kürzlich bekamen sie einen Computer
they recently got a computer

b) *-mal(s)*

ADJECTIVE or NUMERAL	ADVERB
jed- (every)	**jedesmal** (every time)
manch- (many a)	**manchmal** (sometimes)
ein (one)	**einmal** (once)

er hat nur einmal geklopft
he only knocked once

c) *-maßen*

ADJECTIVE	ADVERB
einig- (some)	**einigermaßen** (somewhat)
folgend- (following)	**folgendermaßen** (as follows)

ich war einigermaßen überrascht
I was somewhat surprised

d) *-s*

NOUN	ADVERB
(der) Mittag (midday)	**mittags** (at midday)
(der) Freitag (Friday)	**freitags** (on Fridays)

mittags ißt er in der Kantine
at midday he eats in the canteen

e) *-(er)weise*

-weise can be added to the end of some nouns, **-erweise** to the end of some adjectives:

NOUN *or* ADJECTIVE	ADVERB
(der) Teil (part)	**teilweise** (partly, in parts)
begreiflich (understandable)	**begreiflicherweise** (understandably)

Ihr Aufsatz ist nur teilweise gut
your essay is only good in parts

sie war begreiflicherweise böse auf ihn
she was understandably cross with him

das ist normalerweise nicht der Fall
that's not normally the case

sie hat uns freundlicherweise ihr Auto geliehen
she was very kind and lent us her car

80 ADVERBS

B. USAGE

Adverbs are often used to qualify a verb, but as adverbial intensifiers they can also qualify adjectives and other adverbs.

1. With a verb

morgen schreibt er
he'll write tomorrow

verlassen Sie uns hier?
are you leaving us here?

German usage makes a consistent distinction between position and movement in relation to adverbs. For native speakers of English the greatest difficulty is in translating 'here', 'there' and 'where?'.

wir wohnen hier   *but:*   **sie fährt hierher**
we live here   she's driving here (=to here)

sie saß da/dort   *but:*   **er lief dahin/dorthin**
she was sitting there   he ran there (=to there)

wo arbeiten Sie?   *but:*   **wohin fliegen Sie?**
where do you work?   where are you flying (to)?

wo wartet er?   *but:*   **woher kommt er?**
where is he waiting?   where does he come from?

Note: in conversation the suffixes **-hin** and **-her** often go to the end of the clause:

da gehen wir nie hin!
we never go there!

wo kommen Sie her?
where do you come from?

2. With an adjective

das ist fast einmalig
that's almost unique

ein sehr langweiliges Buch
a very boring book

es war unglaublich kalt
it was unbelievably cold

3. With another adverb

ich koche ebenso gut
I cook just as well

atme schön tief!
breathe nice and deeply!

er schreibt erstaunlich schnell
he writes amazingly quickly

C. WORD ORDER

1. Qualifying an adjective or another adverb

Adverbs come immediately before the adjective or adverb they qualify:

sehr gut
very good/well

ganz hoch
quite tall/high

immer länger
longer and longer

äußerst dünn
extremely thin(ly)

viel lieber
much rather

weiter rechts
further (along) on the right

2. Qualifying a verb

a) In statements the normal position of the adverb is at the end of the clause, but before a past participle, infinitive, separable prefix and, in a subordinate clause, before the finite verb:

Herr Braun liest nicht oft
Mr Braun doesn't read much

sie hat neulich geschrieben
she wrote recently

Sie können mich direkt anrufen
you can dial me direct

ich gebe es sofort auf
I'm giving it up immediately

Note: adverbs of time often occur before a noun in the accusative case:

wir haben heute unsere Weihnachtskarten geschrieben
we've written our Christmas cards today

b) In direct questions the order of the subject and finite verb is reversed, but the normal position of the adverb otherwise remains as in a):

liest Herr Braun nicht oft?
does Mr Braun not often read?

hat sie neulich geschrieben?
has she written recently?

In indirect questions the position of an adverb in the subordinate clause is as in a):

er hat gefragt, ob sie neulich geschrieben hat
he asked if she had written recently

c) In a simple command the normal position of the adverb is after **Sie** and **wir**, or after the finite verb (in the case of the **du** and **ihr** form of the imperative):

bleiben Sie da!   **gehen wir morgen baden!**
stay there!   let's go swimming tomorrow!

fahr langsamer!   **eßt schnell euer Frühstück!**
drive more slowly!   eat your breakfast quickly!

3. Sequence of Adverbs

a) When two or more adverbs (or adverbial phrases) appear in the same sentence, they usually do so in the following sequence:

TIME   MANNER   PLACE

ich bleibe oft alleine zu Hause
I often stay at home by myself

wer fährt diesen Sommer per Anhalter ins Ausland?
who's going hitching abroad this summer?

joggen wir jetzt schnell durch den Park
let's jog fast through the park now

If a cause or reason is included it usually occurs after an expression of time:

er ist gestern wegen der Kälte heimlich ins Kino gegangen
he went to the cinema yesterday in secret because of the cold

Note: with two expressions of time, the more general one comes first:

sie kommen morgen um 5 Uhr an
they're arriving at 5 o'clock tomorrow

b) If several adverbial items are used, it is common for one to be placed at the beginning of the sentence. This may be for special emphasis or for stylistic reasons, since a long string of items can be cumbersome.

ADVERBS

Compare:

> **letzten Montag hat sie ihn aus Eifersucht mit einem Hammer in ihrem Schlafzimmer getötet**
> last Monday she killed him out of jealousy with a hammer in her bedroom

with **aus Eifersucht hat sie ihn letzten Montag mit einem Hammer in ihrem Schlafzimmer getötet**
it was out of jealousy that she killed him last Monday with a hammer in her bedroom

and **mit einem Hammer hat sie ihn letzten Montag aus Eifersucht in ihrem Schlafzimmer getötet**

and **in ihrem Schlafzimmer hat sie ihn letzten Montag aus Eifersucht mit einem Hammer getötet**

D. COMPARATIVES AND SUPERLATIVES

1. Comparative adverbs

a) Comparative adverbs, like comparative adjectives, are formed by adding **-er** to the standard form. This only applies to adverbs with the same standard form as adjectives:

ADVERB	COMPARATIVE ADVERB
einfach (simply)	**einfacher** (more simply)
selten (rarely)	**seltener** (more rarely)
umstritten (controversially)	**umstrittener** (more controversially)

könnten Sie das bitte etwas einfacher ausdrücken?
could you put that a bit more simply, please?

heutzutage kommt das seltener vor
nowadays that happens more rarely

Note: the comparative form of **gern** is **lieber**:

ich trinke gern Cola, aber ich trinke lieber Tee
I like drinking coke, but I prefer to drink tea

For other irregular forms see section C1.

b) 'than' is translated by **als**:

er wächst langsamer als sie
he's growing more slowly than she is

c) **immer** + comparative renders the English comparative + comparative:

seine Stimme klingt immer unangenehmer
his voice sounds more and more unpleasant

sie bleibt immer länger von zu Hause weg
she stays for longer and longer periods away from home

d) 'even' and 'all the' are translated by **noch** and **um so**:

jetzt besuchen sie uns noch häufiger als im Vorjahr
they now visit us even more frequently than last year

nach einer Pause werden wir um so besser arbeiten können
we'll be able to work all the better if we take a rest

2. Superlative adverbs

a) Superlative adverbs are formed by combining **am** with an adverb plus the ending **-sten**. This only applies in the case of adverbs with the same standard form as adjectives:

ADVERB	SUPERLATIVE ADVERB
blöd (stupidly)	**am blödsten** (most stupidly)
selten (rarely)	**am seltensten** (most rarely)
elegant (elegantly)	**am elegantesten** (most elegantly)

von allen hat sie sich am blödsten benommen
she behaved most stupidly of all

die Drossel kommt am seltensten
the thrush comes the most rarely

Note: the superlative form of **gern** is **am liebsten**:

ich reite gern, fahre aber am liebsten Rad
I like riding, but like cycling best

b) When 'most' in English means 'very', rather than implying a comparison, it is usually translated by **höchst**, **äußerst** or **sehr**:

höchst unwahrscheinlich   **äußerst dankbar**
most unlikely   most grateful

das war sehr nett von Ihnen!
that was most kind of you!

6. PRONOUNS

Pronouns are words which can substitute for nouns. They are divided into personal, reflexive, indefinite, relative and interrogative pronouns.

A. PERSONAL PRONOUNS

1. Forms

	NOMINATIVE	ACCUSATIVE	GENITIVE	DATIVE
I	ich	mich	meiner	mir
you	du	dich	deiner	dir
he	er	ihn	seiner	ihm
she	sie	sie	ihrer	ihr
it	es	es	seiner	ihm
we	wir	uns	unser	uns
you	ihr	euch	euer	euch
you	Sie	Sie	Ihrer	Ihnen
they	sie	sie	ihrer	ihnen

2. The translation of 'you'

du is used for the singular when talking to family, friends, children and animals; **ihr** is used for the plural. **Sie** is used when talking to people with whom you are not on '**du**' terms. Nowadays young people often address each other by '**du**' or '**ihr**' even when they are not acquainted. A group containing some people you would call **du** and some you would call **Sie** can quite properly be addressed by **ihr** even though you would revert to **Sie** when talking to one individually. God and saints are addressed by **du**.

hast du die Hausaufgaben?
have you got your homework?

wie heißen Sie, bitte?
what is your name, please?

seid ihr schon zu Hause?
are you home already?

rechts sehen Sie das Schloß
on the right you can see the castle

Note that **du** and **ihr** and all related forms are written with a capital letter at the beginning when used in letter-writing.

3. The use of cases

a) *the nominative*

The nominative is used for the subjects of verbs and following the verb **sein**:

ich sehe	**kannst du kommen?**	
I see	can you come?	

ich bin es	**das sind wir**	**morgen gehen wir**
it's me	that's us	we're going tomorrow

b) *the accusative*

The accusative is used for the direct object of verbs and after certain prepositions (see also p 194-206)

ich mag ihn	**nimm uns mit!**	**ein Brief an dich**
I like him	take us too	a letter to you

Note the use of an accusative object in **wie** ('such as') clauses where it is not used in English:

das sind Berge, wie es sie in meiner Heimat gibt
they are mountains such as we have at home

c) *the genitive*

The genitive of the pronouns is rare and is only used with a small number of verbs, prepositions (see also p 207-9) and adjectives which are followed by the genitive:

erinnerst du dich meiner?	**er war ihrer satt**	**trotz seiner**
do you remember me?	he was tired of her	in spite of him

d) *the dative*

The dative is used for the indirect object of verbs and after certain prepositions (see p 189-93 and 209):

ich gebe es dir	**folgen Sie ihr!**
I'm giving it to you	follow her

nach Ihnen	**bei uns**
after you	at our house

4. Gender

The pronoun has the gender of the noun it replaces. This means that English 'it' will often be translated by **er** or **sie**:

wirf den Stuhl weg, er ist alt
throw the chair away, it's old

diese Tasche ist billig, kauf sie doch!
that bag is cheap, go on, buy it

When a noun that refers to people does not have 'natural' gender the pronoun has the same gender as the 'grammatical' gender of the noun:

und das Kind? − es kommt mit
and the child? − he's/she's coming too

er sah das Opfer, wie es weggetragen wurde
he saw the victim being carried away

but: **das Mädchen** may be referred to as either **es** or **sie**, the latter especially if grown up:

das Mädchen da, kennst du sie?
do you know that girl there?

Note the corresponding use of the possessive adjective **sein**:

das Mädchen spielte mit seiner Puppe
the girl was playing with her doll

5. Special uses of ES

a) **es** can be used as an introductory subject when the noun which is the real subject comes after the verb. Whether the verb is singular or plural depends on the noun. This use sometimes corresponds to the English 'there was...':

es stand ein Mann vor dem Haus
there was a man standing outside the house

es tanzten viele Kinder
a lot of children were dancing

When **es** is used in this way with **sein** it must be remembered that, unlike in English, the verb will be singular or plural depending on the noun following:

es ist deine Freundin   **es sind meine Eltern**
it's your girl friend   it's my parents

Note: with a noun **es** comes before the verb, but with a pronoun the order must be pronoun + verb + **es**:

ach, ihr seid's	**ich bin es**
oh, it's you	it's me

b) **es** is used as the object of **sagen** and **tun** where the English equivalent is 'so':

du hast es gesagt	**ich hoffe, es zu tun**
you said so	I hope to do so

c) **es** is used after the verb **sein** to refer back to a noun or adjective in a preceding clause where in English the verb 'to be' stands alone:

dieser soll besser sein; meinst du, daß er es ist?
this one is supposed to be better; do you think it is?

d) Verbs which are followed by a **daß** clause or a **zu** + infinitive very often have an **es** as object, anticipating the clause or infinitive. There is no equivalent in English:

ich liebe es, alte Filme zu sehen
I love seeing old films

ich kann es nicht verstehen, daß er das vergessen hat
I can't understand how he could have forgotten it

See also the use of **es** for impersonal verbs (p 157-9)

6. The use of pronouns with prepositions

After most prepositions, the third person pronouns (**er**, **sie**, **es**) are usually only used to refer to people:

an sie	**auf ihm**
to her	on him

For a preposition + pronoun referring to an object or idea the form **da(r)-** + preposition is used:

damit	**dagegen**
with it	against it

There is an **-r-** when the preposition begins with a vowel: **daran**, **darauf**, **daraus**, **darin** *etc*:

hast du es daraus genommen?
did you take it out of there?

darin sind wir uns einig	**ich erinnere mich daran**
on that we are agreed	I remember it

This is the case with all prepositions except:

außer	**bis**	**gegenüber**
except	until	opposite
ohne	**seit**	**wider**
without	since	against

and those taking the genitive:

außerhalb	**innerhalb**	**trotz**
outside	within	in spite of
während	**wegen**	and others less
during	because of	common.

For the use of the definite article as an alternative to the personal pronouns see p 22-3.

B. REFLEXIVE PRONOUNS

The reflexive pronouns can be used in the accusative or dative case. The forms are the same as the accusative and dative of the personal pronouns except for the third person and second person in the 'Sie' form:

PERSON	ACCUSATVE	DATIVE
ich	mich	mir
du	dich	dir
er	sich	sich
sie	sich	sich
es	sich	sich
wir	uns	uns
ihr	euch	euch
Sie	sich	sich
sie	sich	sich

Note that the reflexive is the only form of the pronoun where the polite form is not written beginning with a capital.

There is a genitive which has the same forms as the genitive of the personal pronouns. It is used with one or two adjectives, usually together with **selbst**:

> **sie ist ihrer selbst nicht sicher**
> she's not very sure of herself

For the use of the reflexive see p 159-61.

C. INDEFINITE PRONOUNS

Indefinite pronouns substitute for a noun but do not specify precisely to what they refer. Indefinite pronouns are, for example, 'something', 'everyone'.

1. MAN (one, you, people, they, we)

a) *forms*

nom	**man**
acc	**einen**
dat	**einem**

There is no genitive form.

reflexive	**sich**
possessive	**sein**

b) *examples*

heute trägt man keine Hosenträger mehr
people don't wear braces nowadays

man sollte nie sagen, was einem gerade einfällt
you should never say just whatever occurs to you

im Büro hat man mir gesagt ...
they told me in the office...

2. JEMAND (anyone, someone, somebody), NIEMAND (no-one, nobody)

nom	**jemand**	**niemand**
acc	**jemand(en)**	**niemand(en)**
gen	**jemand(e)s**	**niemand(e)s**
dat	**jemand(em)**	**niemand(em)**

The accusative and dative endings are often left out in spoken German and can be left out in written German.

hat jemand nach mir gefragt? **ich habe niemand(en) gesehen**
has anyone been asking for me?   I saw nobody

The reflexive form of **jemand** is **sich**; the possessive adjective used with them is **sein**:

niemand hatte sein Fahrrad dabei
nobody had his/her bicycle with him/her
nobody had their bicycle with them

wenn jemand sich beschwert
if anyone complains

a) **jemand** and **niemand** can be combined with **sonst** (before them) or **anders** (after them) to mean 'someone/no-one else':

   möchte sonst jemand es probieren?
   would someone else like to try?

   niemand anders als sein Bruder
   no-one other than his brother

b) **jemand** can be made even less specific by the addition of **irgend**; they are written as two separate words:

   irgend jemand muß es verloren haben
   someone or other must have lost it

   komm mit irgend jemand
   come with anyone at all

c) **jemand** and **niemand** can be combined with adjectival nouns for phrases of the type of 'somebody interesting' or 'somebody famous'. Although the adjective can have the **-en** ending in the accusative, the following is the commonest form:

nom	**jemand Interessantes**
acc	**jemand Interessantes**
dat	**jemand Interessantem**

   Avoid the genitive by using **von jemand Interessantem**.

3. MEINESGLEICHEN (people like me, of my kind):

meinesgleichen does not change its form according to case:

   sie redet nicht mit meinesgleichen
   she doesn't talk to the likes of me

but forms are possible for all persons: **deinesgleichen, seinesgleichen, unseresgleichen, euresgleichen, Ihresgleichen, ihresgleichen**:

   er redet nur mit seinesgleichen
   he'll only talk to people on his own level

   deinesgleichen kenne ich
   I know your sort

   ein Werk, das seinesgleichen sucht
   a work in a class of its own

4. UNSEREINER (people of our sort, class)

unsereiner is singular; it can have accusative (**unsereinen**) and dative (**unsereinem**) and feminine forms (**unsereine, unsereine, unsereiner**):

unsereiner kann sich das nicht leisten
our sort can't afford that

unsereinem fehlt das Geld dazu
our sort haven't got the money for it

D. UNINFLECTED INDEFINITE PRONOUNS

There is a group of indefinite pronouns which remain the same whatever case they are in:

etwas	**nichts**	**jedermann**
something	nothing	everyone
ein bißchen	**ein paar**	**ein wenig**
a little	a few	a little

ich habe etwas/nichts gehört
I heard something/nothing

nichts war zu hören
nothing was to be heard

mit ein wenig Glück
with a bit of luck

With reflexive verbs they use the reflexive pronoun **sich**; **jedermann** uses the possessive **sein**, **beide** and **ein paar** use **ihr**:

nichts hat sich geändert
nothing has changed

jedermann hat seine Pflicht zu erfüllen
everybody has his duty to do

beide hatten ihre Hausaufgaben nicht gemacht
neither of them had done their homework
both of them had failed to do their homework

1. ETWAS (something)

es war etwas los **hast du etwas gesehen?**
something was going on have you seen something?

etwas is shortened colloquially to **was**:

ich werde dir was zeigen
I'll show you something

etwas can be made even less specific by the addition of **irgend**; they are normally written as two separate words, but **irgendwas** as one:

haben Sie irgend etwas gesehen?
did you see anything at all?

irgendwas muß geschehen sein
something must have happened

etwas can be used as an adjective (it still has no endings) before nouns:

etwas Brot   **ich freue mich auf etwas Ruhe**
some bread   I'm looking forward to some peace and
                        quiet

so etwas is used to mean 'something/anything like that':

hast du je von so etwas gehört?
have you ever heard of anything like it?

so etwas mußte kommen
something like that was bound to happen

etwas is used with **an** + *dat* to translate 'something about':

es ist etwas an ihm, was mir nicht gefällt
there is something about him I don't like

etwas can be used with an adjectival noun for phrases of the type 'something remarkable' or 'something sad'. The adjective has the neuter endings of adjectives with no article (see p 68-71):

das war etwas durchaus Bemerkenswertes
that was something quite remarkable

die Erinnerung an etwas Trauriges
the memory of something sad

wir suchen nach etwas Besserem
we're looking for something better

2. NICHTS (nothing, not anything)

du hast nichts vergessen?
you've not forgotten anything?

ich habe damit nichts zu tun
I have nothing to do with it

a) **nichts** can be intensified by a number of words or phrases to make the equivalent of English 'nothing at all'. All the corresponding German words or phrases come before **nichts**:

gar, ganz und gar, rein gar, überhaupt:

du hast überhaupt nichts getan!
you've done nothing at all

ich habe zu gar nichts Lust
I don't feel like doing anything at all

b) 'nothing else, other than' is usually translated by **sonst nichts**:

da war sonst nichts zu tun
there was nothing else to do

ich brauche sonst nichts als Ruhe
I need nothing except quiet

c) **nichts ander(e)s** is usually the equivalent of 'nothing other than', though the English translation is often 'could only be described as':

das ist nichts ander(e)s als Betrug
that can only be described as fraud

d) **nichts** is used with **an** + *dat* for 'nothing about':

nichts an der Sache gefällt dir
you don't like anything about it

e) **nichts** can be used with an adjectival noun for phrases of the type 'nothing interesting' or 'nothing new'. The adjective has the endings of the neuter adjective without article (see p 68-71):

nichts Interessantes im Fernsehen?
nothing interesting on TV?

3. EIN BISSCHEN (a little), EIN PAAR (a few), EIN WENIG (a little)

These are all used without any change of form of either part. They can be used both by themselves as pronouns and before a noun:

ein paar alte Bekannte   **ein paar werden schon kommen**
a few old friends   a few at least will come

ich möchte ein bißchen frische Luft
I'd like a bit of fresh air

4. JEDERMANN (everyone)

jedermann takes a singular verb. It has no endings except for an **-s** in the genitive:

jedermann hörte den Aufruf
everyone heard the call

das ist nicht jedermanns Sache
that's not everyone's cup of tea

jeder is commoner than **jedermann**; see p 31.

5. BEIDE (both, the two)

beide sind schon da
both are here

a) **beide** can also be used after the definite article, a demonstrative or a possessive; in such cases it has the endings of an adjective after the definite article (see p 65-6) whether it is used before a noun or by itself:

die beiden sind gekommen
the two of them have come

mit diesen beiden neuen Schülern
with these two new pupils

Note the different word order to English:

die beiden Schüler
both the pupils

b) The singular **beides** is a neuter indefinite pronoun which can refer back to two objects or ideas but not to people. It is normally only used in the nominative (**beides**), accusative (**beides**) and dative (**beidem**):

Hut und Mantel, beides hat er vergessen
he's forgotten both his hat and coat

ich bin mit beidem zufrieden
I'm happy with either

beides ist teuer
both are expensive

beides is used with a singular verb except when **sein** is followed by a plural noun:

beides bietet Vorteile	**beides ist richtig**
both have advantages	both are correct

but: **beides sind Erstaufführungen**
both are first performances

c) **beide** is only used in the plural and can refer to both people and objects:

> | | |
> |---|---|
> | *nom* | **beide** |
> | *acc* | **beide** |
> | *gen* | **beider** |
> | *dat* | **beiden** |

>   **beide wollen kommen**
>   both (of them) want to come

>   **beide waren gleich teuer**
>   both (of them) were just as expensive

d) *Word order:* **beide** can be used alone before the verb or come later in the sentence when a noun or pronoun is subject:

> | | |
> |---|---|
> | **beide wollen kommen** | **sie wollen beide kommen** |
> | both want to come | they both want to come |

>   **die Mädchen wollen beide kommen**
>   the girls both want to come

>   **leider kommen die Mädchen beide**
>   unfortunately both of the girls are coming

>   **leider kommen beide Mädchen**
>   unfortunately both girls are coming

e) **beide** can be emphasised by having **alle** before it:

> | | |
> |---|---|
> | **sind alle beide gekommen?** | **ihr seid Schurken, alle beide!** |
> | have both of them come? | you're rascals, the two of you! |

f) **beide** after personal pronouns:

>   The endings of **beide** can vary when it is used after personal pronouns. In general, **beide** has the same endings as plural adjectives with no article before (see p 68-71):

> | | |
> |---|---|
> | **wir beide** | **für euch beide** |
> | both of us | for the two of you |

>   **sie beide zusammen**
>   the two of them together

except: after **ihr** and between **ihr** or **wir** and a noun:

> | | |
> |---|---|
> | **ihr beiden** | **ihr beiden Freunde** |
> | both of you | you two friends |

>   **wir beiden alten Gammler**
>   we two old layabouts

100 PRONOUNS

Note: Many other types of word can be used as indefinite pronouns. For the use as indefinite pronouns of: the indefinite article, the possessives, **derjenige**, **derselbe**, **dieser**, **jeder**, **keiner**, **mancher**, **welcher**, **alles**, **alle** *(plural)* and **solche** *(plural)* see the individual entries in the section on articles p 28-36. For **welcher** see p 34-6.

E. ADJECTIVES USED AS PRONOUNS

1. A number of adjectives can be used without a following noun, ie as a pronoun. They generally have the normal adjective endings according to gender, number, case and whether they are preceded by an article or not:

    gestern war ein anderer da
    another person was there yesterday

    folgendes muß getan werden
    the following must be done

    It is often difficult to distinguish these from adjectival nouns; for when not to use a capital, see p 45.

2. Some adjectives are most commonly used as indefinite pronouns in the plural

a) **einige** ('some, several'), **mehrere** ('several'), **viele** ('much, many') and **wenige** ('little, few') are the commonest:

    ich habe einige schon bemerkt
    I've noticed several already

    der beste unter vielen
    the best of many

    nur wenige sind erschienen
    only a few turned up

    er kennt die Arbeiten mehrerer
    he knows several people's work

b) All (except **mehrere**) can also used by themselves, as pronouns, in the singular, but with certain restrictions.

   i) **einiges**

      As a singular pronoun, **einiges** is only used as a neuter collective, not referring to people; its usual English equivalent is 'some things':

      einiges, was ihm neu war
      some things which were new to him

      ich habe einiges mitgebracht
      I've brought a few things with me

Like **etwas** and **nichts**, it can be used before adjectival nouns:

einiges Interessante
a few interesting things

ii) **viel** and **wenig** can have the neuter endings (**vieles**, **vielem**) but are most commonly used without endings:

wir haben viel von ihm gehört
we've heard a lot about him

nur wenig gelang ihm
not much turned out right for him

aus wenig macht er viel
he turns a little into a lot

The forms with endings are commoner in the dative:

von vielem enttäuscht
disappointed with many things

viel and **wenig** are very commonly used with adjectival nouns. The commoner form is to use **viel**, **wenig** without endings, the adjectival noun having the endings of a neuter adjective with no article before:

viel Überflüssiges	**neben wenig Ausgezeichnetem**
much that is superfluous	alongside little that was excellent

3. **sämtlich** ('all without exception') is generally used as a normal adjective but it can be used without ending and following the verb to emphasize completeness:

sie waren sämtlich erschienen
they all came, every one

F. RELATIVE PRONOUNS

The relative pronoun introduces a subordinate clause. It refers back to a preceding noun, pronoun or clause about which the relative clause provides further information or definition. For example, in the sentence, 'the man who did it', 'who' refers back to 'the man' and the clause 'who did it' tells us more about him.

As these are subordinate clauses, in German the verb goes at the end.

1. Forms

German generally uses the definite article for the relative pronoun.

	MASCULINE	FEMININE	NEUTER	PLURAL ALL GENDERS
nom	der	die	das	die
acc	den	die	das	die
gen	dessen	deren	dessen	deren
dat	dem	der	dem	denen

Note the change in form from the definite article for the genitive and dative plural.

welche is also used as a relative pronoun; see p 36.

2. Agreement

In English the relative pronouns 'which' and 'that' have only one form; 'who' has an accusative form 'whom' and a genitive 'whose'

In German the form varies according to number, gender or case. The German relative pronoun takes its gender and number from what it refers back to, but its case from its function (subject, object *etc*) in the relative clause. For example, in the sentence:

der Junge, den ich gestern sah
the boy that I saw yesterday

der Junge is masculine singular; in the relative clause he is what was seen, ie the object; therefore the masculine singular accusative of the relative pronoun is used.

der Spieler, der gewonnen hat
the player who won

der Betrag, den du zahlen mußt
the amount you have to pay

die Lehrer, denen er es erklären muß
the teachers he has to explain it to

die Frau, deren Mann du kennst
the woman whose husband you know

der Mann, dessen Frau du kennst
the man whose wife you know

Note: the relative pronoun can never be omitted in German as it sometimes is in English:

die Frau, die du kennst
the woman you know

3. Use with prepositions

a) Prepositions always come before the relative pronoun, never at the end of the sentence as they sometimes do in English:

die Hausaufgabe, von der du weißt
the homework that you know about

der Zug, mit dem er reist
the train he'll be travelling on

b) When the relative pronoun used with a preposition doesn't refer back to a person but to an object or idea, then the form **wo(r)** + preposition is frequently also used. *Compare*:

die Ansagerin, von der er sprach
the announcer he spoke about

and: **das Thema, worüber er sprach**
das Thema, über das er sprach
the subject he spoke about

The form **wor-** is used with prepositions that begin with a vowel.

4. The alternative neuter form WAS

was is normally used for the neuter nominative and accusative to refer back to the following:

a) *indefinite neuter pronouns* such as **alles, etwas, nichts** (for list see above p 95):

nichts, was mich interessierte
nothing that I was interested in

etwas, was mir Sorgen machte
something that worried me

einiges, was ich bedenken sollte
some things I should consider

When **das** is used instead of **was**, especially after **etwas**, it is because the speaker has something specific in mind. *Compare*:

gibt es irgend etwas, was ich tun kann?
is there anything I can do?

and: **er sah etwas, das ihn schockierte**
he saw something that shocked him

b) *a neuter adjectival noun:*

das Beste, was du tun kannst
the best you can do

das meiste, was ich gelesen habe
the most that I have read

c) *a whole clause:*

er sagte ab, was alle bedauerten
he called off, which everyone regretted

die Regierung trat zurück, was Neuwahlen erforderlich machte
the government resigned, which led to a general election

Note: **was** is not used with a preposition:

er rutschte aus, worüber alle lachten
he slipped, which made everyone laugh

5. Replacement of the relative pronoun by WO (where)

a) Clauses of place are often introduced by the conjunction **wo** ('where') instead of the preposition + relative pronoun:

ein Land, wo er viel Zeit verbrachte
a country in which he spent a lot of time

b) When the relative refers back to the name of a country, town or place, **wo** must be used instead of preposition + relative pronoun:

Rom, wo es so viele schöne Kirchen gibt
Rome where there are so many fine churches

c) **wo** is also often used in place of a preposition + relative pronoun in clauses of time:

die Jahre, wo er viel verdiente
the years in which he earned a lot

die Woche, wo ich verreist war
the week in which I was away

6. WER as a relative

The interrogatives **wer** and **was** (for forms see below) can each be used as a relative, without implying a question, when the relative clause starts a sentence and is the subject of the main verb. The English equivalent is usually 'anyone who' or 'whoever':

wer das kauft, muß schwachsinnig sein
whoever buys that must be daft

wer wagt, gewinnt	**wem der Mut fehlt, darf gehen**
he who dares wins	anyone who lacks the courage may go

G. INTERROGATIVE PRONOUNS

1. There are two interrogative pronouns, one for persons (**wer**) and one for things (**was**):

	PERSONAL	IMPERSONAL
nom	**wer**	**was**
acc	**wen**	**was**
gen	**wessen**	**wessen**
dat	**wem**	-

   wer kommt heute?
   who's coming today?

   was sagst du?
   what do you say?

   wessen Mantel ist das?
   whose coat is that?

   mit wem geht sie aus?
   who is she going out with?

   auf wen kann ich rechnen?
   who can I count on?

2. They are all usually singular, but take a plural of the verb **sein** if followed by a plural noun:

   wer sind deine Begleiter?
   who are your companions?

   was sind seine Gründe?
   what are his reasons?

3. Use with prepositions

   When used with a preposition, **was** is replaced by the **wo(r)** + preposition forms of the relative pronoun:

   womit soll ich es waschen?
   what shall I wash it with?

   woran liegt das?
   what's the cause of it?

4. When the clause introduced by the interrogative pronoun follows a verb of saying, asking or similar it is a subordinate clause (an indirect question) and the verb therefore goes to the end:

   weißt du, wer heute kommt?
   do you know who's coming today?

   erzähl mir, was er gesagt hat
   tell me what he said

   For the alternative use of **welcher?** as an interrogative pronoun see p 34-5.

H. THE ORDER OF PRONOUNS

For a fuller treatment see p 228-30.

1. Pronouns as direct and indirect objects generally come immediately after the verb:

> **ich gebe dir das Geld**
> I'll give you the money
>
> **ich habe ihm das Buch geliehen**
> I lent him the book

a) When there are two pronoun objects the order is accusative before dative:

> **habe ich es dir gegeben?**
> did I give it to you?
>
> **ich habe es ihm geliehen**
> I lent it to him

b) The same order applies when one is a dative reflexive:

> **er kann es sich nicht leisten**
> he can't afford it

c) Otherwise the reflexive generally comes immediately after the verb:

> **er kauft sich einen Filzstift**
> he's buying a felt-tip

2. A pronoun subject must come immediately after the verb when there is an inversion:

> **morgens macht sie ihm das Frühstück**
> in the mornings she makes his breakfast for him
>
> **gestern hat sie ihn gesehen**
> she saw him yesterday

3. A noun subject can come before or after a pronoun object:

> **gestern hat ihn meine Schwester gesehen**
> **gestern hat meine Schwester ihn gesehen**
> my sister saw him yesterday

7. VERBS

The section on verbs is divided into the following:
A Verb types and forms
B Notes on verb forms
C Use of tenses
D Conjugation tables

A. VERB TYPES AND FORMS

1. Types of verbs

There are two main types of verb in German, generally referred to as weak and strong verbs. Weak verbs conform to a group pattern with a few standard variations. Strong verbs have a common basic pattern but a much greater degree of variation within it so that the main parts have to be learnt for each individual verb. There is a small number of verbs of mixed type. For a list of the main parts of strong and mixed verbs, see p 118-24 and 128-9.

The fundamental difference between the two types is in the formation of the imperfect tense and the past participle: the weak verbs add a characteristic **-t-** to the verb stem (= infinitive without **-(e)n** ending) in these forms; strong verbs change the stem vowel of the infinitive when forming the imperfect tense and past participle, for example:

		imperfect	past participle
weak:	**packen**	**ich packte**	**gepackt**
strong:	**singen**	**ich sang**	**gesungen**

These two basic types are similar to the two basic verb types in English (from the examples above, English pack – packed – packed and sing – sang – sung). This similarity of verb form between English and German is very helpful in learning German verbs – but it does not always apply. However, if an English and German verb have the same root (eg **packen** - to pack, **singen** - to sing, **sagen** - to say, **lieben** - to love) the likelihood is that they will both be of the same type. Exceptions such as **helfen** (strong) and 'to help' (weak) should warn one to check if in doubt.

VERBS

By far the largest number of verbs belong to the weak group. New creations are always weak (eg **managen** − **gemanagt**) and some verbs originally strong are gradually adopting weak forms (eg **stecken** ['to be in a situation'] imperfect **stak** often replaced by weak **steckte**). Many strong verbs, however, are very common verbs, eg **sein** ('to be'), **gehen** ('to go') *etc*.

2. Tenses, moods and voices

a) *main tenses:*

　i) present
　ii) imperfect
　iii) perfect
　iv) pluperfect
　v) future
　vi) future perfect

b) *moods:*

　i) indicative
　ii) imperative
　iii) subjunctive
　iv) conditional

c) *voices:*

　i) active
　ii) passive

d) *the infinitive*

The form in which the verb is usually given in dictionaries is called the infinitive. It consists of the verb stem plus **(e)n**. It is the equivalent of the English form with to: to read = **lesen (les + en)**.

VERBS

3. Verb forms: the conjugation of verbs

a) *weak verbs*

   i) Present tense

   The present tense is formed by adding the endings **-e**, **-st**, **-t**, **-en**, **-t**, **-en** to the stem.

infinitive	**fragen**	**reden**	**heizen**
ich	**frage**	**rede**	**heize**
du	**fragst**	**redest**	**heizt**
er/sie/es	**fragt**	**redet**	**heizt**
wir	**fragen**	**reden**	**heizen**
ihr	**fragt**	**redet**	**heizt**
Sie/sie	**fragen**	**reden**	**heizen**

infinitive	**atmen**	**klingeln**	**plaudern**
ich	**atme**	**klingle**	**plaud(e)re**
du	**atmest**	**klingelst**	**plauderst**
er/sie/es	**atmet**	**klingelt**	**plaudert**
wir	**atmen**	**klingeln**	**plaudern**
ihr	**atmet**	**klingelt**	**plaudert**
Sie/sie	**atmen**	**klingeln**	**plaudern**

haben is a weak verb but has slightly irregular forms:

ich	**habe**
du	*hast*
er/sie/es	*hat*
wir	**haben**
ihr	**habt**
Sie/sie	**haben**

Standard variations:

★ An **-e-** is inserted before the **-st** and **-t** endings for verbs whose stem ends in **-t** or **-d**: see **reden** above; and for verbs whose stem ends in an **-m** or **-n** (but not **-mm**, **-nn**, **-lm**, **-ln**, **-rm** or **-rn**): see **atmen** above; **filmen** ('to film') would not need the extra **-e-**.

★ In verbs whose stem ends in **-s**, **-ß**, **-x**, **-z** the s of **-st** ending is omitted (see **heizen** above).

★ Verbs whose infinitive ends in **-eln** lose the **e** before the **l** in the **ich** form (see **klingeln** above); this can also happen in verbs ending in **-ern** but is not obligatory (see **plaudern** above).

112 VERBS

ii) Imperfect tense

The imperfect tense is formed by adding the endings **-te**, **-test**, **-te**, **-ten**, **-tet**, **-ten** to the stem.

infinitive	**fragen**	**reden**	**atmen**
ich	fragte	redete	atmete
du	fragtest	redetest	atmetest
er/sie/es	fragte	redete	atmete
wir	fragten	redeten	atmeten
ihr	fragtet	redetet	atmetet
Sie/sie	fragten	redeten	atmeten

haben loses the **-b-** of the stem in the imperfect tense:

ich	hatte
du	hattest
er/sie/es	hatte
wir	hatten
ihr	hattet
Sie/sie	hatten

★ Standard variations

In verbs whose stems end in **-d** or **-t**, or in **-m** or **-n** (but not **-mm**, **-nn**, **-lm**, **-ln**, **-rm** or **-rn**) an **e** is inserted between the stem and the ending (see **reden**, **atmen** above).

iii) Perfect tense

The perfect tense is formed by using the past participle (for the formation of the past participle see section xiv below) with the present tense of **sein** or **haben**. For the question of whether to use **sein** or **haben** see p 131-3 below.

fragen		**reisen**	
ich habe	gefragt	ich bin	gereist
du hast	gefragt	du bist	gereist
er/sie/es hat	gefragt	er/sie/es ist	gereist
wir haben	gefragt	wir sind	gereist
ihr habt	gefragt	ihr seid	gereist
Sie/sie haben	gefragt	Sie/sie sind	gereist

The participle normally comes at the end of the sentence or clause.

VERBS

iv) Pluperfect tense

The pluperfect is formed by using the past participle (for the formation of the past participle see section xiv below) together with the imperfect tense of **sein** or **haben**. For the question of whether to use **sein** or **haben** see p 131-3 below.

fragen	**reisen**
ich hatte............. gefragt	ich war .... gereist
du hattest .... gefragt	du warst .... gereist
er/sie/es hatte ..... gefragt	er/sie/es war ...... gereist
wir hatten .... gefragt	wir waren .... gereist
ihr hattet .... gefragt	ihr wart .... gereist
Sie/sie hatten........ gefragt	Sie/sie waren ...... gereist

The participle normally comes at the end of the sentence or clause.

v) Future tense

The future is formed by using the present tense of **werden** plus the infinitive:

fragen

ich werde .... fragen
du wirst .... fragen
er/sie/es wird......... fragen
wir werden .... fragen
ihr werdet .... fragen
Sie/sie werden ...... fragen

The infinitive normally comes at the end of the sentence or clause.

vi) Future perfect

The future perfect is formed by using the present tense of **werden** plus the perfect infinitive (see section xv below). For the question of whether to use **sein** or **haben** see p 131-3 below.

fragen	**reisen**
ich werde .... gefragt haben	ich werde .... gereist sein
du wirst .... gefragt haben	du wirst .... gereist sein
er/sie/es wird ... gefragt haben	er/sie/es wird ... gereist sein
wir werden ... gefragt haben	wir werden .... gereist sein
ihr werdet .... gefragt haben	ihr werdet .... gereist sein
Sie/sie werden ... gefragt haben	Sie/sie werden ...... gereist sein

114 VERBS

vii) Imperative mood (for usage and alternative forms see p 141-2 below)

There are imperatives for the **du**, **ihr**, **Sie** and **wir** forms of the verb. The imperative of the **du** form is the stem of the verb to which an **-e** is sometimes added; the others have the same endings as in the indicative. The **du** and **ihr** forms are normally used without a pronoun, the **Sie** and **wir** forms retain the pronoun but with inversion.

It is usual in German to have an exclamation mark at the end of an imperative.

fragen	entschuldigen	klingeln
frag(e)!	entschuldige!	klingle!
fragen wir!	entschuldigen wir!	klingeln wir!
fragt!	entschuldigt!	klingelt!
fragen Sie!	entschuldigen Sie!	klingeln Sie!

The **-e** of the second person singular is normally left off, especially in spoken language; it is quite correct to omit it in written German. It is retained for verbs ending in **-igen** (see **entschuldigen** above).

Those ending in **-eln**, **-ern** normally omit the e of the stem and retain the final **-e** (see **klingeln** above).

Verbs whose stem ends in two different consonants retain the **-e** for reasons of ease of pronunciation (eg **atme!**, **antworte!**); verbs with a stem ending in **-d** or **-t** often keep the **-e** (**red!** or **rede!**, **bet!** or **bete!**).

viii) Present subjunctive

The present subjunctive is formed by adding the following endings to the verb stem: **-e**, **-est**, **-e**, **-en**, **-et**, **-en**.

fragen	haben
ich frage	ich habe
du fragest	du habest
er/sie/es frage	er/sie/es habe
wir fragen	wir haben
ihr fraget	ihr habet
Sie/sie fragen	Sie/sie haben

haben is regular in the present subjunctive.

ix) Imperfect subjunctive

The imperfect subjunctive for weak verbs is the same as the imperfect indicative (see section ii above).

haben has an umlaut in the imperfect subjunctive:

ich hätte
du hättest
er/sie/es hätte
wir hätten
ihr hättet
Sie/sie hätten

x) Perfect and pluperfect subjunctives

The perfect and pluperfect subjunctives are formed in the same way as the perfect and pluperfect tenses except that the present or imperfect subjunctive of **sein** or **haben** is substituted for the present or imperfect indicative.

fragen	**reisen**
ich habe/hätte .... **gefragt**	**ich sei/wäre** .... **gereist**
du habest/hättest ...... **gefragt**	**du sei(e)st/wär(e)st** ...... **gereist**
er habe/hätte .... **gefragt**	**er sei/wäre** .... **gereist**
wir haben/hätten ...... **gefragt**	**wir seien/wären** .... **gereist**
ihr habet/hättet ...... **gefragt**	**ihr seiet/wär(e)t** .... **gereist**
Sie/sie haben/hätten .. **gefragt**	**Sie/sie seien/wären** ...... **gereist**

xi) Conditional: the subjunctive formed with **würde**

Very often the standard present, imperfect and perfect subjunctives are replaced by a compound form using the imperfect subjunctive of **werden** plus the infinitive or the perfect infinitive:

fragen

ich würde..................... **fragen**
du würdest .... **fragen**
er/sie/es würde .... **fragen**
wir würden .... **fragen**
ihr würdet .... **fragen**
Sie/sie würden............... **fragen**

ich würde .... **gefragt haben**
du würdest .... **gefragt haben**
er/sie/es würde .... **gefragt haben**
wir würden .... **gefragt haben**
ihr würdet .... **gefragt haben**
Sie/sie würden ...... **gefragt haben**

xii) Passives

There are two forms of the passive in German, one using the auxiliary **werden**, the other using **sein**, both with the past participle of the verb. For a distinction of the usage see p 140-1 below.

passive with **werden**   passive with **sein**

ich werde .... **gefragt**	**ich bin** .... **gefragt**
du wirst .... **gefragt**	**du bist** .... **gefragt**
er/sie/es wird .... **gefragt**	**er/sie/es ist** .... **gefragt**
wir werden .... **gefragt**	**wir sind** .... **gefragt**
ihr werdet .... **gefragt**	**ihr seid** .... **gefragt**
Sie/sie werden .... **gefragt**	**Sie/sie sind** .... **gefragt**

More complex tenses can be formed by using the other tenses of **werden** with the past participle:

imperfect passive:

ich wurde .... **gefragt** *etc*

perfect passive:

ich bin .... **gefragt worden** *etc*

Note the special form of the past participle of **werden** used to form the passive.

pluperfect passive:

ich war ...... **gefragt worden** *etc*

future passive:

ich werde ..... **gefragt werden** *etc*

future perfect passive:

ich werde gefragt worden sein *etc*

Passive subjunctives can also be formed by using the subjunctive of **werden**.

xiii) Present participle

The present participle is formed by adding **-d** to the infinitive. For usage see p 151.

xiv) Past participle

The past participle is formed from the verb stem plus **(e)t** and normally begins with the prefix **ge-**:

gefragt   geatmet   geheizt   geredet

★ The final **t** is preceded by an **e** in verbs whose stem ends in **-d** or **-t** or in a consonant preceded by a different consonant except for **l** and **r**.

★ In separable verbs the **ge-** is placed between the separable prefix and the verb stem eg **ausgefragt, zurückgereist, eingeatmet**.

★ The prefix **ge-** is omitted in verbs with an inseparable prefix and verbs ending in **-ieren**:

besucht	**verletzt**	**übernachtet**
erwartet	**vollendet**	**telefoniert**

This also includes separable verbs ending in **-ieren** or formed on a verb which already has an inseparable prefix:

einstudiert   **anerkannt**

★ Verbs which can be separable or inseparable (see p 136) can have two past participles:

übersetzt	**übergesetzt**
translated	ferried over

xv) Infinitive

The infinitive is the basic form of the verb in which it is given in dictionaries etc. It always ends in **-(e)n** and does not change its form, but different tenses of the infinitive can be created by combining it with other parts of the verb:

infinitive	**sehen** (to see)
perfect infinitive	**gesehen haben** (to have seen)
passive infinitive	**gesehen werden** (to be seen)
passive infinitive	**gesehen sein** (to be seen)
perfect infinitive passive	**gesehen worden sein** (to have been seen)

118 VERBS

b) *strong verbs*

   i) Present tense

The present tense is formed by adding the endings **-e**, **-(e)st**, **-(e)t**, **-en**, **-(e)t**, **-en**. In some verbs the vowel of the stem changes in the second and third person singular.

infinitive	**finden**	**sehen**	**fahren**
ich	finde	sehe	fahre
du	findest	siehst	fährst
er/sie/es	findet	sieht	fährt
wir	finden	sehen	fahren
ihr	findet	seht	fahrt
Sie/sie	finden	sehen	fahren

infinitive	**stoßen**	**gehen**	**werfen**
ich	stoße	gehe	werfe
du	stößt	gehst	wirfst
er/sie/es	stößt	geht	wirft
wir	stoßen	gehen	werfen
ihr	stoßt	geht	werft
Sie/sie	stoßen	gehen	werfen

infinitive	**sein**	**werden**	**bitten**
ich	bin	werde	bitte
du	bist	wirst	bittest
er/sie/es	ist	wird	bittet
wir	sind	werden	bitten
ihr	seid	werdet	bittet
Sie/sie	sind	werden	bitten

Note: **sein** is completely irregular in the present tense.

★ the extra **-e-** is added to the **du**, **er/sie/es** and **ihr** forms for verbs whose stems end in **-d** or **-t**, except when there has been a vowel change. Compare **finden**, **bitten** above with:

    laden > lädst   **raten > rätst**   **schelten > schiltst**
    schmelzen > schmilzt   **treten > trittst**

★ The commonest changes of stem vowel in the **du** and **er/sie/es** forms are:

a > ä: see **fahren** above. Almost all strong verbs with stem vowel **a** modify it to **ä**, except **schaffen**; **backen** is nowadays commonly found without an umlaut and with a weak imperfect tense.

e (short) > **i**: see **werden**, **werfen** above. Most verbs with stem vowel **e** (short) modify to **i**.

e (long) > **ie**: see **sehen** above. This is most common when **e** is followed by **h**:

befehlen > befiehlt	gebären > gebiert
geschehen > geschieht	lesen > liest

ii) Imperfect tense

Most strong verbs change the stem vowel for the imperfect tense; there is no ending added for the **ich** and **er/sie/es** forms; all the others have the same endings as the present tense.

infinitive	pfeifen	finden	bleiben
ich	pfiff	fand	blieb
du	pfiffst	fandst	bliebst
er/sie/es	pfiff	fand	blieb
wir	pfiffen	fanden	blieben
ihr	pfifft	fandet	bliebt
Sie/sie	pfiffen	fanden	blieben

infinitive	schließen	helfen	sein
ich	schloß	half	war
du	schlossest	halfst	warst
er/sie/es	schloß	half	war
wir	schlossen	halfen	waren
ihr	schloßt	halft	wart
Sie/sie	schlossen	halfen	waren

★ In the imperfect tense the **-e-** inserted after verb stems that end in **-d**, **-t** etc is felt to be particularly stilted. It is almost never inserted in spoken German and is normally avoided in written German except for the **du** forms of verbs whose stem ends in **-s**, **-sch**, **-x**, **-z** (see **schließen** above) and for the **ihr** forms of verbs with stem ending in **-d** and **-t** (see **finden** above)

★ For a list of strong verbs in the imperfect, see p 166-71.

★ Some verbs have a change in the final consonant of the stem, eg **ziehen** > **ich zog**. See the list on p 166- 71.

★ werden

werden has an irregular imperfect tense as it changes the vowel but adds the weak endings (the older, strong form – **ich ward**, **du ward(e)st**, **er ward** in the singular – will occasionally be met in older literary works):

ich wurde
du wurdest
er/sie/es wurde
wir wurden
ihr wurdet
Sie/sie wurden

iii) Perfect tense

The perfect tense is formed by using the past participle (formation of past participle see section xiv) with the present tense of **sein** or **haben**. For the question of whether to use **sein** or **haben** see p 131-3:

fahren	finden
ich bin .... gefahren	**ich habe** .... gefunden
du bist .... gefahren	**du hast** .... gefunden
er/sie/es ist .... gefahren	**er/sie/es hat** ...... gefunden
wir sind .... gefahren	**wir haben** .... gefunden
ihr seid .... gefahren	**ihr habt** .... gefunden
Sie/sie sind .... gefahren	**Sie/sie haben** ... gefunden

The participle normally comes at the end of a sentence or clause.

iv) Pluperfect tense

The pluperfect tense is formed by using the past participle (for the formation of the past participle see section xiv below) with the imperfect tense of **sein** or **haben**. For the question of whether to use **sein** or **haben**, see p 131-3 below.

fahren	finden
ich war .... gefahren	**ich hatte** .... gefunden
du warst .... gefahren	**du hattest** .... gefunden
er/sie/es war ...... gefahren	**er/sie/es hatte** .. gefunden
wir waren .... gefahren	**wir hatten** .... gefunden
ihr wart .... gefahren	**ihr hattet** .... gefunden
Sie/sie waren ...... gefahren	**Sie/sie hatten** ... gefunden

The past participle normally comes at the end of the sentence or clause.

VERBS 121

v) **Future tense**

The future tense is formed by using the infinitive with the present tense of **werden**:

fahren

ich werde .... fahren
du wirst .... fahren
er/sie/es wird .... fahren
wir werden .... fahren
ihr werdet .... fahren
Sie/sie werden ...... fahren

The infinitive normally comes at the end of the sentence or clause.

vi) **Future perfect**

The future perfect is formed by using the perfect infinitive (ie the past participle with the infinitive of **sein** or **haben**) with the present tense of **werden**. For the question of whether to use **sein** or **haben** see p 131-3.

fahren		**finden**	
ich werde	.... gefahren sein	ich werde	...... gefunden haben
du wirst	.... gefahren sein	du wirst	...... gefunden haben
er/sie/es wird	... gefahren sein	er/sie/es wird	.gefunden haben
wir werden	...... gefahren sein	wir werden	... gefunden haben
ihr werdet	...... gefahren sein	ihr werdet	... gefunden haben
Sie/sie werden	... gefahren sein	Sie/sie werden	gefunden haben

vii) **Imperative** (for usage and alternative forms see p 141-2)

There are imperatives for the the **du**, **ihr**, **Sie** and **wir** forms of the verb alone. The **du** form is the stem of the verb to which an **-e** is sometimes added; the others have the same endings as in the indicative. The **du** and **ihr** forms are normally used without a pronoun, the **Sie** and **wir** forms retain the pronoun but with inversion.

It is usual in German to have an exclamation mark at the end of an imperative.

fahren

fahr(e)!
fahren wir!
fahrt!
fahren Sie!

122 VERBS

★ The **-e** ending of the **du** form is normally left off, especially in spoken German; it is quite correct to omit it in written German.

★ Verbs which change the stem vowel from **e** to **i** in the **du** form of the indicative also have the change in the imperative:

sehen
sieh(e)!
sehen wir!
seht!
sehen Sie!

but: Verbs which change from **a** to **ä** do not have the change in the imperative (see **fahren** above).

Note: The **du** form of the imperative of **werden** is **werde!**

★ The imperative of **sein**:

sei!
seien wir!
seid!
seien Sie!

viii) Present subjunctive

The present subjunctive is formed by adding the following endings to the stem **-e**, **-est**, **-e**, **-en**, **-et**, **-en**. No verbs change the stem vowel.

Infinitive	**fahren**	**sehen**
ich	**fahre**	**sehe**
du	**fahrest**	**sehest**
er/sie/es	**fahre**	**sehe**
wir	**fahren**	**sehen**
ihr	**fahret**	**sehet**
Sie/sie	**fahren**	**sehen**

ix) Imperfect subjunctive

The imperfect subjunctive is formed by adding the endings **-e**, **-est**, **-e**, **-en**, **-et**, **-en** to the stem of the imperfect tense. If the vowel of the stem is **a**, **o**, or **u** it always has an umlaut.

fahren	bleiben	sein
ich führe	ich bliebe	ich wäre
du führest	du bliebest	du wär(e)st
er/sie/es führe	er/sie/es bliebe	er/sie/es wäre
wir führen	wir blieben	wir wären
ihr führet	ihr bliebet	ihr wär(e)t
Sie/sie führen	Sie/sie blieben	Sie/sie wären

x) Perfect and pluperfect subjunctives

The perfect and pluperfect subjunctives are formed in the same way as the perfect and pluperfect indicatives (see sections iii and iv above) except that the present or imperfect subjunctive of **sein** or **haben** is substituted for the present or imperfect indicative.

fahren		finden	
ich sei/wäre	.... gefahren	ich habe/hätte	.... gefunden
du sei(e)st/wär(e)st	... gefahren	du habest/hättest	...... gefunden
er sei/wäre	.... gefahren	er habe/hätte	.... gefunden
wir seien/wären	...... gefahren	wir haben/hätten	...... gefunden
ihr seiet/wär(e)t	...... gefahren	ihr habet/hättet	...... gefunden
Sie/sie seien/wären	... gefahren	Sie/sie haben/hätten	gefunden

xi) Conditionals or subjunctives with **würde**

As for weak verbs. See section axi above.

xii) Passives

As for weak verbs. See section axii above.

xiii) Present participle

As for weak verbs. See section axiii above.

xiv) Past participle

The past participle is formed from the verb stem (usually with a change of vowel) which is normally preceded by the prefix **ge-** and followed by **-en**:

fahren	>	gefahren	bleiben	>	geblieben
werfen	>	geworfen	singen	>	gesungen

★ The past participle of **sein** is **gewesen**

124 VERBS

★ In separable verbs the **ge-** is placed between the prefix and the verb stem:

    einschlafen > eingeschlafen   **aussteigen > ausgestiegen**

★ The **ge-** is omitted in verbs that have an inseparable prefix:

    verstehen > verstanden   **empfehlen > empfohlen**

c) *modal verbs*

  i) Present tense

  The present tense has no endings on the verb stem in the **ich** and **er/sie/es** forms; the ending for **du** is **-st**, those for **wir**, **ihr** and **Sie/sie -en**, **-t**, **-en**. The vowel of the verb stem in the singular is different from that of the infinitive and plural forms, except for **sollen**.

infinitive	dürfen	können	mögen
ich	durfte	konnte	mochte
du	durftest	konntest	mochtest
er/sie/es	durfte	konnte	mochte
wir	durften	konnten	mochten
ihr	durftet	konntet	mochtet
Sie/sie	durften	konnten	mochten

infinitive	müssen	sollen	wollen
ich	muß	soll	will
du	mußt	sollst	willst
er/sie/es	muß	soll	will
wir	müssen	sollen	wollen
ihr	müßt	sollt	wollt
Sie/sie	müssen	sollen	wollen

  ii) Imperfect tense

  The imperfect tense is formed with the same endings as weak verbs (see p 112) but there is a change of stem vowel, except for **sollen** and **wollen**.

infinitive	dürfen	können	mögen
ich	durfte	konnte	mochte
du	durftest	konntest	mochtest
er/sie/es	durfte	konnte	mochte
wir	durften	konnten	mochten
ihr	durftet	konntet	mochtet
Sie/sie	durften	konnten	mochten

VERBS

infinitive	müssen	sollen	wollen
ich	mußte	sollte	wollte
du	mußtest	solltest	wolltest
er/sie/es	mußte	sollte	wollte
wir	mußten	sollten	wollten
ihr	mußtet	solltet	wolltet
Sie/sie	mußten	sollten	wollten

Note the change of consonant in **mögen**.

iii) Perfect and pluperfect tenses

The perfect and pluperfect tenses are formed using **haben**. When the six modal verbs are used in their commonest function as auxiliary verbs the infinitive is used instead of the past participle:

ich habe/hatte ...... **gehen dürfen**
du hast/hattest ...... **gehen dürfen**
er/sie/es hat/hatte ... **gehen dürfen**
wir haben/hatten ... **gehen dürfen**
ihr habt/hattet ...... **gehen dürfen**
Sie/sie haben/hatten **gehen dürfen**

The modal verbs also have a regular past participle formed in the same way as those of weak verbs except that those that have an umlaut lose it:

gedurft gekonnt gemocht gemußt gesollt gewollt.

These regular past participles are rarely used.

★ There is another form of the perfect tense using the present indicative of the modal verbs with the perfect infinitive of the verb, that is the past participle plus the infinitive of **sein** or **haben**:

ich kann ... **gesehen haben**   **ich muß** ... **gefahren sein**
du kannst ... **gesehen haben**   **du mußt** ... **gefahren sein**
etc

For the distinction in sense between these two forms see p 156-7.

126 VERBS

iv) Future tense

The future tense is formed by the present tense of **werden** plus the infinitive of the main verb plus the infinitive of the modal:

ich werde .... **kommen können**
du wirst .... **kommen können**
er/sie/es wird ...... **kommen können**
wir werden .... **kommen können**
ihr werdet .... **kommen können**
Sie/sie werden ... **kommen können**

v) Future Perfect

The future perfect is formed by the present tense of **werden** plus the perfect infinitive of the main verb and the infinitive of the modal. This clumsy form is almost never used. A sentence such as:

sie glaubt nicht, daß ich es bis morgen werde geschrieben haben können

is less common than the equivalent English form:

she doesn't think I will have been able to write it by tomorrow

The simpler form:

sie glaubt nicht, daß ich es bis morgen geschrieben habe

expresses practically the same idea.

vi) Imperative

There is no imperative form of the modals.

vii) Present subjunctive

The present subjunctive is formed by adding the following endings to the infinitive stem: **-e, -est, -e, -en, -et, -en**.

ich könne
du könnest
er/sie/es könne
wir können
ihr könnet
Sie/sie können

VERBS 127

viii) Imperfect subjunctive

The imperfect subjunctive is the same as the imperfect indicative, except that those modal verbs which have an umlaut on the stem vowel in the infinitive also have it in the imperfect subjunctive:

ich	könnte	möchte	wollte
du	könntest	möchtest	wolltest
er/sie/es	könnte	möchte	wollte
wir	könnten	möchten	wollten
ihr	könntet	möchtet	wolltet
Sie/sie	könnten	möchten	wollten

Note the change of consonant in **mögen**.

ix) Perfect subjunctive

There are two forms of the perfect subjunctive.

One is formed with the present subjunctive of **haben** plus the infinitive of the main verb plus the infinitive of the modal:

ich habe .... **sehen können**
du habest .... **sehen können**
er/sie/es habe .... **sehen können**
wir haben .... **sehen können**
ihr habet .... **sehen können**
Sie/sie haben .... **sehen können**

The other is formed by using the present subjunctive of the modal with the past infinitive of the main verb:

ich könne........	**gesehen haben**	**ich müsse**.........	**gefahren sein**
du könnest	**gesehen haben**	**du müssest**	**gefahren sein**
er/sie/es könne .	**gesehen haben**	**er/sie/es müsse** ..	**gefahren sein**
wir können	**gesehen haben**	**wir müssen**	**gefahren sein**
ihr könnet	**gesehen haben**	**ihr müsset**	**gefahren sein**
Sie/sie können ..	**gesehen haben**	**Sie/sie müssen** ...	**gefahren sein**

128 VERBS

x) **Pluperfect subjunctive**

There are two forms of the pluperfect subjunctive.

One is formed with the imperfect subjunctive of **haben** plus the infinitive of the main verb plus the infinitive of the modal:

ich hätte .... **sehen können**
du hättest .... **sehen können**
er/sie/es hätte ... **sehen können**
wir hätten .... **sehen können**
ihr hättet .... **sehen können**
Sie/sie hätten ... **sehen können**

The other is formed by using the imperfect subjunctive of the modal with the perfect infinitive of the main verb (see p117):

ich könnte ...	**gesehen haben**	**ich müßte**	**gefahren sein**
du könntest ...	**gesehen haben**	**du müßtest** ...	**gefahren sein**
er/sie/es könnte	**gesehen haben**	**er/sie/es müßte**	**gefahren sein**
wir könnten ...	**gesehen haben**	**wir müßten** ...	**gefahren sein**
ihr könntet ...	**gesehen haben**	**ihr müßtet** ...	**gefahren sein**
Sie/sie könnten	**gesehen haben**	**Sie/sie müßten**	**gefahren sein**

d) *verbs of mixed type*

i) A group of verbs has the endings of the weak conjugation but changes the stem vowel from **-e-** in the infinitive and present to **-a-** in the imperfect tense and past participle. Apart from this vowel change, they are perfectly regular weak verbs. They are: **brennen, kennen, nennen, rennen**.

infinitive	present	imperfect	past participle
brennen	**ich brenne**	**ich brannte**	**gebrannt**
kennen	**ich kenne**	**ich kannte**	**gekannt**
etc			

The imperfect subjunctive is also irregular:

ich brennte   **ich kennte**
etc

ii) Two verbs which can form their parts in this way can also have a regular weak imperfect and past participle:

infinitive	present	imperfect	past participle
senden	**ich sende**	**ich sandte**	**gesandt**
	etc	**ich sendete**	**gesendet**
wenden	**ich wende**	**ich wandte**	**gewandt**
	etc	**ich wendete**	**gewendet**

They have only one imperfect subjunctive form which is the same as the regular weak imperfect indicative.

Note the difference in meaning for **senden**:

senden (regular weak verb) = to broadcast
(mixed verb) = to send

Both forms can be used for most meanings of **wenden**; the form with vowel change being slightly more literary. **wenden** meaning 'to turn' in sewing must have the regular forms.

iii) **denken** and **bringen** change both the vowel and final consonant of the stem in the imperfect and past participle but have regular weak endings eg

infinitive	present	imperfect	past participle
bringen	**ich bringe**	**ich brachte**	**gebracht**
denken	**ich denke**	**ich dachte**	**gedacht** *etc*

The imperfect subjunctive is:

        ich brächte   **ich dächte**   *etc*

iv) **wissen**

wissen forms its main tenses in a similar way to the modal verbs:

present
    ich weiß
    du weißt
    er/sie/es weiß
    wir wissen
    ihr wißt
    Sie/sie wissen

imperfect
    ich wußte
    du wußtest
    er/sie/es wußte
    wir wußten
    ihr wußtet
    Sie/sie wußten

past participle   **gewußt**

present subjunctive
    ich wisse
    du wissest
    er/sie/es wisse
    wir wissen
    ihr wisset
    Sie/sie wissen

imperfect	**ich wüßte**
subjunctive	**du wüßtest**
	er/sie/es wüßte
	wir wüßten
	ihr wüßtet
	Sie/sie wüßten

v) A small number of verbs have parallel weak and strong forms, sometimes with a difference in sense between the two forms. Many are not commonly needed for everyday use but two commoner examples are noted here:

bewegen (bewegte, bewegt) = to move
bewegen (bewog, bewogen) = to persuade someone (to do something)

schaffen (schaffte, geschafft) = to do, achieve
schaffen (schuf, geschaffen) = to create

vi) some verbs have a combination of strong and weak forms:

mahlen − mahlte − gemahlen

salzen − salzte − gesalzen

In some cases a more modern weak form is replacing an older strong one:

backen − backte (*older:* **buk**) **− gebacken**

B. NOTES ON VERB FORMS

1. The formation of compound tenses with *haben* or *sein*

a) *haben* is used

   i) with all transitive verbs, ie verbs that can take an object:

   er hat die Wurst gegessen
   he ate the sausage

   This applies even where the verb is used without an object:

   er hat schon gegessen
   he has already eaten

Note: the few exceptions are transitive verbs formed by adding a prefix to a verb that normally takes **sein**:

   er ist seinen Husten noch nicht losgeworden
   he hasn't got rid of his cough yet

   ii) with all reflexive verbs:

   hast du dich schon gewaschen?
   have you washed yet?

   iii) with modal verbs:

   mein Sohn hat den Film nicht sehen können
   my son couldn't see the film

   das habe ich nicht gewollt
   that wasn't part of my intention

   solche Musik habe ich immer gemocht
   I've always liked that kind of music

   iv) with impersonal verbs:

   es hat geregnet
   it rained

★ except:

gelingen	mißlingen	glücken	mißglücken
geschehen	passieren	vorkommen	widerfahren

   es ist ihm gelungen   **es ist schon passiert, daß ...**
   he succeeded   it's happened before that ...

132 VERBS

- ★ except impersonal expressions with verbs that normally take **sein**:

    wie ist es dir ergangen?
    how did you get on?

- v) with intransitive verbs denoting action:

    du hast aber fleißig gearbeitet
    you have been working hard

b) *sein is used:*

- i) with intransitive verbs expressing change of place, state or situation. The nost frequently used verbs of this type are those expressing motion from one place to another:

    er ist nach Hause gegangen **das Geld ist verschwunden**
    he has gone home   the money's disappeared

    das Haus ist abgebrannt
    the house has burnt down

- ii) with the verbs listed as exceptions of aiv above, whether used impersonally or not:

    der Plan ist mißglückt
    the plan failed

- iii) with **sein** and **werden** used both as auxiliary verbs and as full verbs:

    das wäre besser gewesen   **die Milch ist sauer geworden**
    that would have been better   the milk has gone off

    der Vorschlag ist akzeptiert worden
    the suggestion has been accepted

c) *verbs which may take either **sein** or **haben***

- i) Note that many verbs of motion can form their perfect tense with **sein** or **haben**, depending on the sense. Motion from one place to another requires **sein**, motion seen as a way of spending time takes **haben**:

    sie sind nach Griechenland gesegelt
    they sailed to Greece

    im Urlaub hat er jeden Tag gesegelt
    on holiday he went sailing every day

There is a modern tendency not to make this distinction:

wir sind über den See geschwommen
we swam across the lake
and:
wir sind den ganzen Tag geschwommen
we swam all day
instead of:
wir haben den ganzen Tag geschwommen
we swam all day

The latter is still perfectly correct, however.
Verbs with which this distinction in usage between **sein** and **haben** is still normally kept are:

paddeln	**reiten**	**rudern**	**segeln**	**tanzen**
to paddle	to ride	to row	to sail	to dance

ii) Some verbs of motion can be used both transitively and intransitively; in the first case they are conjugated with **haben**, in the second with **sein**:

gestern hat er den Wagen gefahren
he drove the car yesterday
sie ist nach Hause gefahren
she drove home

er hat das Rohr gebogen	**sie ist um die Ecke gebogen**
he bent the pipe	she went round the corner

iii) Note similar distinctions:

er ist mir gefolgt	**er hat mir gefolgt**
he followed me	he obeyed me
der See ist gefroren	**ich habe gefroren**
the lake has frozen	I was freezing

iv) As a rule, **liegen**, **sitzen** and **stehen** are conjugated with **haben** in north Germany, with **sein** in south Germany and Austria.

134 VERBS

2. The order of infinitives and past participles

a) In tenses formed with an auxiliary verb – **sein, haben, werden** and the modals – the auxiliary verb comes in second position in the sentence but the past participle and/or infinitive comes at the end of the clause:

wir sind gestern gefahren   **das kann ich nicht sagen**
we travelled yesterday   I can't say

es wird gerade gebaut
it's just being built

b) If there is both past participle and infinitive, the past participle comes first:

sie werden früher gefahren sein
they must have gone earlier

c) The infinitive of a modal verb used as a past participle and the past participle of **werden** come after the infinitive or past participle of the main verb:

das hättest du voraussehen können
you should have foreseen that

es ist noch nicht gebaut worden
it hasn't been built yet

d) In the future perfect passive the past participle is followed by **worden** and then **sein**:

es wird sicher bis Montag gefunden worden sein
I'm sure it will have been found by Monday

e) In the future perfect plus a modal the past participle is followed by the infinitive of **sein** or **haben** and then the infinitive of the modal:

er wird es gefunden haben müssen
he will have had to have found it

Note: these last two forms are often regarded as clumsy (see p 126)

f) Special word order in subordinate clauses

When two infinitive forms occur in a subordinate clause then the finite verb comes before them:

weißt du, daß ich dich habe kommen sehen?
do you know I saw you coming?

er sagte, daß er mich nicht hat verstehen können
he said he hadn't been able to understand me

3. Prefixes

a) *inseparable*

The inseparable prefixes are:

be-   emp-   ent-   er-   ge-   miß-   ver-   zer-

In pronunciation they are not stressed. They never separate from the verb. A verb with such a prefix has no **ge-** in the past participle.

b) *separable*

i) All other common prefixes are separable with the exception of the group mentioned in c) below. When they are attached to the verb they are stressed in pronunciation.

In statements, questions and imperatives these prefixes separate from the verb and are placed at the end of the clause. This does not apply in subordinate clauses where the finite verb is also at the end and prefix and verb are joined:

kommst du mit?   **kommen Sie mit!**
are you coming?   come with me

sie fangen an   *but:* **weißt du, wann sie anfangen?**
they're beginning   do you know when they begin?

ii) The past participle for verbs with a separable prefix is formed with the **ge** coming between the prefix and verb stem:

anfangen – angefangen   beibringen – beigebracht

iii) When a verb with a separable prefix is in the infinitive form and is used with **zu** the **zu** comes between the prefix and the verb stem:

er versuchte, den Weg abzukürzen
he tried to take a short cut

um die Zeit gut auszunutzen
so as to make good use of the time

136 VERBS

c) *separable or inseparable*

> **durch- hinter- über- um- unter- wider- voll-**

can be either separable or inseparable prefixes. In most such cases the separable and inseparable verbs have different meanings:

> **der Gärtner gräbt den Dung unter**
> the gardener digs the dung in

but:

> **er untergräbt seine Gesundheit**
> he is undermining his health

Usually the separable verb has a concrete, physical meaning, the inseparable verb a figurative meaning.

d) *double prefixes*

  i) In verbs which already have an inseparable prefix to which a separable one is added (eg **ab-be-rufen**) the separable prefix still separates, the **zu** is inserted between separable and inseparable prefix *but* the past participle has no **ge-**:

> **die Regierung beruft den Botschafter ab**
> the government recalls its ambassador
>
> **die Regierung beabsichtigt, den Botschafter abzuberufen**
> the government intends to recall its ambassador
>
> **der Botschafter wurde abberufen**
> the ambassador was recalled

  wieder is always separable except in **wiederholen** in the sense of 'to repeat':

> **ich habe sie nie wiedergesehen**
> I never saw her again
>
> **sie wiederholten die Lektion**
> they repeated the lesson

  ii) Verbs formed by the combination of inseparable prefix + separable prefix + verb (eg **be-ab-sichtigen**) are inseparable:

> **er beabsichtigt, morgen zu kommen**
> he intends to come tomorrrow

C. USE OF TENSES

1. The present tense

a) The present tense is used

   i) to express present states or actions:

   ich fühle mich schlecht
   I feel ill

   der Arzt gibt mir eine Spritze
   the doctor is giving me an injection

   ii) to express general or universal truths:

   Sabine hört gern Rockmusik   **Zeit ist Geld**
   Sabine likes rock music   time is money

   iii) for firm intentions, refusals and for orders as an alternative to the imperative:

   ich mache das
   I'll do it

   ich bleibe keine Minute länger hier!
   I won't stay here a minute longer

   das Auto springt nicht an
   the car won't start

   du gehst sofort ins Bett!
   you're to go to bed at once

Note: it is often translated by either the English present or the present continuous:

   es regnet jeden Tag   **es regnet**
   it rains every day   it is raining

b) In German the present tense is the commonest way of expressing the future:

   ich bin gleich zurück   **nächste Woche ist alles vorbei**
   I'll be right back   it'll all be over by next week

   du bekommst einen Brief
   you'll be getting a letter

138 VERBS

c) With the conjunctions **seit** and **seitdem** and adverbial phrases using the preposition **seit** the present tense is used to express actions or states starting in the past and continuing into the present:

> **seit(dem) er die Tabletten nimmt, geht es ihm viel besser**
> since he has been taking the tablets he has been much better
>
> **er wartet seit zehn Uhr**
> he has been waiting since ten o'clock

d) The historic present is commoner in German than in English. It is used to enliven a narrative of past events in written or spoken German:

> **ich liege auf der Couch — da kommt der Peter und gießt mir Wasser über den Kopf**
> there I was lying on the sofa when in came Peter and poured water over my head

It is also used for for newspaper headlines and historical notes:

> **DIE QUEEN BESUCHT BONN**
> THE QUEEN VISITS BONN
>
> **1814: Napoleon entkommt aus der Haft**
> 1814: Napoleon escapes

2. The imperfect tense

a) The imperfect tense is the standard tense for stories, novels and newspaper reports.

> **er ging die Straße entlang**
> he went along the road
>
> **der sowjetische Außenminister traf gestern in Bonn ein**
> the Soviet foreign secretary arrived in Bonn yesterday

b) The imperfect tense is the one most commonly used (less so in southern Germany) with **sein**, **haben** and the modal verbs when referring to the past:

> **das war klasse!**   **ich konnte es kaum glauben**
> that was great!   I could hardly believe it

c) Note the following use of the imperfect with **seit(dem)**:

> **seit(dem) er in Hamburg wohnte, hatte er ...**
> since he had been living in Hamburg, he had ...

VERBS

3. The perfect tense

The perfect tense is the standard tense for conversation when talking about the past (with the exception of the use of **haben**, **sein** and the modals as shown in 2.):

hast du ihn gesehen? **wann ist sie angekommen?**
did you see him? when did she arrive?

This does not mean to say that the imperfect cannot be used in German conversation. If, for example, you are relating a series of events then it is quite in order to use the imperfect (it's like telling a story). But for single utterances as in the above two examples, the use of the imperfect would sound odd.

4. The pluperfect tense

The pluperfect is used for events that happened before a particular time in the past:

nachdem wir den Film gesehen hatten, gingen wir ins Café
after we had seen the film we went to a café

5. The future and future perfect tenses

a) The future is used to express future matters but is less common in German than in English (see 1b above). The future as in:

ich werde ihn morgen treffen
I'm going to meet him tomorrow

is very often expressed by the present:

ich treffe ihn morgen
I'm meeting him tomorrow

b) It is also used to express suppositions about the present:

er hört mich nicht, er wird das Radio an haben
he can't hear me, he's probably got the radio on

c) The future perfect is used to refer to an event that will be completed at some stage in the future:

ich werde das Buch bis Montag gelesen haben
I'll have read the book by Monday

It is also commonly used in German to express a supposition as in b) above:

> **er wird es vergessen haben**
> he'll have forgotten it

6. The passive

In the passive the active form ('he does it') is turned round so that the object becomes subject ('it was done by him').

a) There are two forms of the passive in German: the passive of action and the passive of state. The first (formed with **werden**) emphasises the action that was carried out, the second (formed with **sein**) denotes the result:

> **die Vase wurde zerbrochen**   **die Vase ist zerbrochen**
> the vase was broken   the vase is broken

When an agent is mentioned (who it was done by) the passive formed with **werden** must be used:

> **diese Wohnungen werden von der Stadt gebaut**
> these flats are being built by the council

but: **unser Haus ist schon gebaut**
our house is already built

b) Verbs that take the dative or that are followed by a preposition cannot form the passive in this way and so a passive construction is usually avoided. For example:

> he was followed by them
> **sie sind ihm gefolgt**

When a passive is used with such verbs note the difference from English:

> *mir* **wurde gesagt**
> *I* was told

c) Intransitive verbs can be transformed into an impersonal passive in which there is commonly no agent expressed:

> **es wurde getanzt**
> there was dancing

d) The agent (the subject of the verb in its active form) is usually referred to by the preposition **von**:

> **er wurde von seinem besten Freund betrogen**
> he was betrayed by his best friend

durch is most often used when the agent is not a person:

> **die Ernte wurde durch Hagel vernichtet**
> the harvest was destroyed by hail
>
> **ich wurde durch den Verkehr aufgehalten**
> I was held up by traffic

e) Note the use of **man** to replace a passive construction where a sentence such as 'it had been completely forgotten about' can be expressed either by

> **es war völlig vergessen worden**

or by

> **man hatte es völlig vergessen**

f) The passive can also be expressed by lassen:

> **das läßt sich machen** **er ließ sich nicht überreden**
> that can be done he couldn't be persuaded

g) The infinitive with **zu** can also be used to express the passive:

> **wie ist das zu erklären?** **er war nicht zu verstehen**
> how is that to be explained? he couldn't be understood

7. The imperative

a) The imperative is used to express requests and can range from a peremptory demand to a polite suggestion:

> **bleiben Sie stehen!** **komm doch her!**
> stop come here
>
> **sieh dir den kleinen Bengel an!** **hören Sie nicht auf!**
> just look at the little rascal don't stop

There is normally an exclamation mark, even after polite requests.

b) In the **wir** form, it is used for suggestions:

> **gehen wir!** **machen wir es uns gemütlich!**
> let's go let's make ourselves comfortable

142 VERBS

c) The infinitive is an alternative imperative, usually for fairly peremptory commands, for example in road signs *etc*:

links fahren!   **nicht hinauslehnen!**
drive on the left   do not lean out

8. The subjunctive

a) In spite of the fact that certain forms of the subjunctive are felt to be stilted (and are often replaced by the indicative or the **würde** form), it is still widely used in German:

  i) in conversation for conditional statements and with the modal verbs and:

  ii) in formal German, eg news bulletins, for reported statements.

  The subjunctive gives the verb a mood of uncertainty, improbability or unreality. Thus it is mainly used for conditional statements, to express what might have been or what might, but probably will not, be; and for reported speech where it shows that what is reported was said by someone else and the speaker is not guaranteeing its truth or otherwise.

b) The use of the subjunctive in conditional sentences

  i) Conditional sentences contain a main clause and an 'if' (**wenn**) clause. Conditional clauses in the present tense do not require the subjunctive; they state what will happen if some condition is fulfilled:

  wenn es morgen regnet, arbeite ich zu Hause
  if it rains tomorrow, I'll work at home

  ii) Conditions with the imperfect subjunctive in the main clause and in the **wenn** clause suggest the condition is unlikely to be fulfilled:

  wenn ich mehr Zeit hätte, ginge ich öfter spazieren
  if I had more time, I would go for more walks

iii) The use of the **würde** forms

The verb in the example above could be replaced by a **würde** form:

wenn ich mehr Zeit hätte, würde ich öfter spazierengehen

This does not normally occur with **sein** and **haben**.

Note the possibility of omitting the **wenn** with inversion of subject and verb:

hätte ich mehr Zeit, ginge ich öfter spazieren

iv) Conditions with the pluperfect subjunctive in both clauses are matters that might have happened but did not:

wenn er mich gefragt hätte, hätte ich ihm das Geld geliehen
if he had asked me, I would have lent him the money

The substitution of **würde** forms is also possible here, though less common.

v) A **wenn** clause with the subjunctive can be used by itself in the sense of 'if only':

wenn es nur schon Weihnachten wäre
if only it were Christmas

c) The subjunctive with **als ob** and **als wenn**

The **als ob** or **als wenn** ('as if') construction expresses something which is regarded as uncertain or misleading and normally has the subjunctive, although in spoken German the indicative can be used:

er tut, als ob er uns nicht gesehen hätte
he behaves as if he hadn't seen us

d) The subjunctive can be used in a main clause alone for instructions in mathematics and cookery:

man nehme fünf Eier
take five eggs

and with **leben** meaning 'long live' or 'three cheers for'

es lebe die Revolution!   **er lebe hoch!**
long live the revolution   three cheers for him

144 VERBS

e) The subjunctive can also be used for questions and requests to make them less blunt and therefore more polite:

ich hätte eine Frage
might I ask a question?

hätten Sie fünf Minuten für mich?
could you spare me five minutes?

f) The subjunctive can be used for suggestions in the phrase **wie wäre es mit ...** ('how about ...?'):

wie wär's mit einem Glas Wein
how about a glass of wine

g) For the idiomatic uses of the subjunctive of modal verbs, see the section on modal verbs below.

h) The subjunctive in indirect speech

  i) Indirect speech is when a statement or question spoken by one person is reported by someone else:

  he said, "I will go there" > he said he would go there

  The indirect speech is usually contained in a clause following a verb of speaking or asking. In German, such clauses are the only ones where the introductory **daß** may be omitted; if there is no **daß** they keep the normal word order:

  er sagte, daß er kommen würde
  he said he would come

  er sagte, er würde kommen
  he said he would come

  ii) Indirect speech without the subjunctive

  In German, direct speech is usually put into indirect speech by using the subjunctive, but if the verb of saying or asking is in the present tense, then the indicative is more common:

  er sagt, daß er kommt
  he says he's coming

  In colloquial German the subjunctive is often avoided and the indicative retained in the tense used in direct speech:

  er hat gesagt, daß er kommt
  he said he would come

iii) Indirect speech with the subjunctive

The choice of tense for the indirect statement depends on the tense of the original direct speech as shown in the following table:

indicative tense of direct speech	subjunctive tense of indirect speech
present	present, imperfect
imperfect, perfect or pluperfect	perfect, pluperfect
future	future, **würde** + infinitive

Examples

ich finde es schwierig	**er hat gesagt, er finde/fände es schwierig**
I find it difficult	he said he found it difficult
ich fand es schwierig	
ich habe es schwierig gefunden	**er hat gesagt, er habe/hätte es schwierig gefunden**
ich hatte es schwierig gefunden	
ich werde es schwierig finden	**er hat gesagt, er werde/würde es schwierig finden**

iv) The choice of subjunctive tense in indirect speech

★ Written German

The preferred tenses in formal written German are the present subjunctive, the imperfect subjunctive and the future subjunctive (the first ones given in each of the examples above).

The main exceptions occur when the form of the subjunctive is identical to the indicative form it is replacing. In such cases the alternative form given above is used:

sie sagten, sie fänden (*not* **finden**) **es schwierig**

sie sagten, sie hätten (*not* **haben**) **es schwierig gefunden**

sie sagten, sie würden (*not* **werden**) **es schwierig finden**

If the present and imperfect subjunctives are both the same as the indicatives, the imperfect subjunctive is preferred:

sie sagten, sie arbeiteten (*not* **arbeiten**) **fleißig**

146 VERBS

★ **Spoken German**

The preferred tenses in spoken German are the imperfect subjunctive, pluperfect subjunctive and **würde** + infinitive forms (the second choices given in the examples above).

The **würde** + infinitive form is very commonly used instead of the imperfect subjunctive for verbs other than **sein** and **haben**:

sie sagte: "Ich wohne hier" > sie sagte, sie würde hier wohnen
she said, "I live here"   she said she lived here

9. The uses of the infinitive

The infinitive can be used together with certain verbs without any connecting link; in all other cases it is connected to the verb, noun or adjective phrase with **zu**.

a) *the infinitive without zu*

The infinitive is used without **zu** with modal verbs, and with certain verbs of perception, causation and instruction:

dürfen	to be allowed to
können	to be able to
mögen	to like to
müssen	to have to
sollen	to be supposed to
wollen	to want to
fühlen	to feel
hören	to hear
sehen	to see
spüren	to feel
heißen	to order to
lassen	to make, cause to; to allow to
machen	to make
helfen	to help to
lehren	to teach to
lernen	to learn to

i) modals

ich darf das nicht tun   er will es gesehen haben
I'm not allowed to do that   he claims to have seen it

das muß heute getan werden
it has to be done today

ii) The verbs of perception, causation and instruction normally have an object (in the dative with **helfen**) as well as the infinitive:

er fühlte sein Herz schlagen **hörst du ihn kommen?**
he felt his heart beating can you hear him coming?

ich sah ihn fallen
I saw him fall

er spürte eine Wut in sich aufsteigen
he felt his anger rising

er hieß die Soldaten warten (*literary German*)
he told the soldiers to wait

sie ließ die Schüler früh nach Hause gehen
she allowed the children to go home early

Montag lasse ich den Wagen waschen
on Monday I'll get the car washed

er machte die Leute aufhorchen
he made the people sit up and listen

sie haben mir aufräumen geholfen
they helped me tidy up

wer hat dich schwimmen gelehrt?
who taught you to swim?

er lernt gerade Auto fahren
he's just learning to drive

Note: when **helfen**, **lehren** and **lernen** are followed by an infinitive which has its own object or an adverb with it, the tendency is to use **zu**.

Compare:

der Blindenhund hilft ihm gehen
the guide dog helps him to walk

and: **der Blindenhund hilft ihm, die Straße zu überqueren**
the guide dog helps him to cross the road

iii) The infinitive after **lassen** (and less commonly after **sehen**, **hören** and **heißen**) often has a passive sense:

er ließ das Zimmer streichen
he had the room painted

Compare this with the following use of **lassen**:

er ließ mich das Zimmer streichen
he got me to paint the room

lassen is used in this way as a reflexive (see p 161):

das läßt sich machen
that can be done

iv) After **bleiben**, verbs of sitting, standing, lying *etc* are in the infinitive without **zu**:

bleib sitzen!	**er blieb auf dem Boden liegen**
stay seated	he remained lying on the ground

v) **brauchen** is normally used with **zu** + infinitive in standard German but is also sometimes used without **zu**, especially in spoken German:

das brauchst du nicht an(zu)nehmen
you don't have to accept that

vi) **kommen**, **gehen** and **schicken** are used without **zu** with verbs denoting activities:

kommst du morgen schwimmen?
are you coming swimming tomorrow?

er hat die Kinder einkaufen geschickt
he sent the children out shopping

Note: Past participle

When **heißen**, **lassen**, **sehen** and **hören** are used together with another infinitive, then it is normal to use the infinitive forms (**heißen, lassen, sehen, hören**) rather than the past participle forms (**geheißen, gelassen, gesehen, gehört**):

er hat mich kommen sehen	**er hat das Feuer ausgehen lassen**
he saw me coming	he let the fire go out

Note: Special word order

In subordinate clauses the finite verb precedes two infinitives at the end of a sentence:

weil er dich hat kommen lassen
because he got you to come

VERBS 149

b) *the infinitive with* **zu**

- i) After nouns:

    hast du Lust mitzuspielen?
    would you like to join in the game?

- ii) After adjectives:

    ich war froh, ihn gesehen zu haben
    I was glad to have seen him

- iii) After past participles:

    er war erstaunt, mich zu sehen
    he was astonished to see me

- iv) After the prepositions **um**, **(an)statt**, and **ohne**:

    um ... zu is used to express purpose:

    er zahlte mehr, um einen besseren Platz zu bekommen
    he paid more to get a better seat

    um ... zu is also used after **genug** ('enough') and **zu** ('too') + adjective:

    du bist alt genug, um das zu wissen
    you're old enough to know that

    er ist zu schwach, um nein zu sagen
    he's too weak to say no

    (an)statt zu ('instead of'):

    (an)statt zu feuern, ließ er die Waffe fallen
    he dropped his gun instead of shooting

    ohne zu ('without')

    er ging vorbei, ohne zu grüßen
    he went past without saying hello

Note: after nouns, adjectives, past participles and prepositions the subject of the main verb must also be the subject of the infinitive.

VERBS

- v) After verbs:

    es begann sofort zu regnen **wir versuchten ihn aufzuhalten**
    it immediately started to rain we tried to stop him

    Verbs which are followed by a preposition often, but not always, have **da(r)** + preposition before the **zu** + infinitive phrase:

    ich freue mich darauf, euch zu sehen
    I'm looking forward to seeing you

    er ärgerte sich (darüber), den Zug verpaßt zu haben
    he was annoyed at missing the train

    After **sein** the infinitive with **zu** has a passive meaning:

    er ist nicht zu ersetzen **der Schmerz war nicht zu ertragen**
    he is irreplaceable the pain was unbearable

- vi) Punctuation

    If the infinitive phrase has any other elements, such as an object or adverb, then a comma is placed between the main clause and the infinitive phrase; otherwise there is no comma.

    er versuchte zu laufen
    he tried to run

    er versuchte, über die Straße zu laufen
    he tried to run across the road

c) For the use of the infinitive as imperative see section 7c above.

d) The infinitive can also be used as a noun. Such nouns begin with a capital letter and are always neuter; they generally denote the action of the verb:

   das Schwimmen
   swimming

   They can be compounded with a noun object:

   das Autofahren
   car driving

   They are often used with **bei**:

   er wurde beim Mogeln ertappt
   he was caught cheating

10. The uses of the participles

a) *present participle*

   i) The present participle is used mainly as an adjective either before the noun or after **sein**:

   eine ansteckende Krankheit **diese Krankheit ist ansteckend**
   an infectious disease this disease is infectious

   ii) It can occasionally be used as an adverb after other verbs:

   sie redete überzeugend
   she talked convincingly

   iii) The present participle preceded by **zu** - which can have further words or phrases before it — can be used as an extended adjective before the noun:

   kein einfach zu lösendes Problem
   a problem that is not easy to solve

   eine schwer zu begreifende Entscheidung
   a decision that is/was difficult to comprehend

   iv) Phrases using present participles in the following way are mainly literary usage:

   die Zeitung zerknüllend, stand er auf
   crumpling the paper, he stood up

b) *past participle*

   i) Apart from its use to form tenses, the past participle is also used as an adjective:

   der verdammte Bengel
   that damned boy

   ii) Its use to form extended adjective phrases before the noun is widespread in formal written German:

   der erst neulich gestürzte Präsident
   the recently deposed president

   iii) Phrases using past participles in the following way are mainly literary usage:

152 VERBS

vom Einbruch der Nacht überrascht, mußte er im Freien schlafen
being suddenly overtaken by nightfall, he had to sleep out of doors

but: a small number of verbs are in common use in such participial constructions, for example: **vorausgesetzt**, **gesagt**, **ausgenommen**:

genau gesagt
to be precise

dein Bruder ausgenommen, fahren alle mit dem Zug
except for your brother everyone is going by train

iv) The past participle is used idiomatically with **kommen**:

er kam gelaufen
he came running

11. The usages of modal verbs (conjugation see p 124-8)

a) *dürfen*

i) **dürfen** expresses permission ('to be allowed to'):

niemand darf das Haus verlassen
no-one may leave the house

darf ich Sie stören?	**das darfst du nicht sagen**
may I interrupt	you shouldn't/mustn't say that

ii) **dürfen** in the imperfect subjunctive expresses a probable supposition:

er dürfte gestern krank gewesen sein
he was probably ill yesterday

das dürfte wohl stimmen
that might well be true

iii) **dürfen** in the negative translates English 'must not':

du darfst nicht bei Rot über die Straße gehen
you must not cross the road when the lights are red

iv) Idiomatic uses:

was darf es sein?
(in shop) what can I do for you?
(getting a drink) what can I get you?

b) **können**

   i) **können** expresses ability:

   er kann gut schwimmen
   he can swim well

   kannst du Gitarre spielen?
   do you know how to play the guitar?

   leider können wir nicht kommen   **kannst du Spanisch?**
   I'm afraid we can't come   can you speak Spanish?

   ii) **können** expresses possibility:

   er kann den Einbrecher gesehen haben
   he might have seen the burglar

   du kannst recht haben
   you might be right

   iii) **können** is often used in place of **dürfen** to express permission, especially in spoken German:

   du kannst machen, was du willst
   you can do as you like

   iv) **können** is used in the idiom **etwas/jemand (gut) leiden können**:

   ich kann diese Musik gut leiden
   I like this music

c) **mögen**

Note: **mögen** is also used with an object, meaning 'to like':

   ich mag keine Rockmusik
   I don't like rock music

   i) The commonest use of **mögen** is to express wish or desire. In this usage it is most often seen in the imperfect subjunctive:

   ich möchte ihn kennenlernen   **ich möchte ein Eis**
   I'd like to get to know him   I'd like an ice cream

   but it is also used in the present:

   ich mag nicht länger bleiben
   I don't want to stay any longer

154 VERBS

    ii) **mögen** is used to express supposition or possibility:

        du magst recht haben   **wer mag das sein?**
        you may well be right   who can/might that be?

        er mochte etwa zwanzig sein
        he was probably about twenty

    iii) **mögen** expresses concession:

        das mag sein, aber es gefällt mir nicht
        that may be so, but I don't like it

    iv) The imperfect subjunctive of **mögen** is also used as a polite alternative to the imperative:

        Besucher möchten das Schloß bitte vor sechs Uhr verlassen
        visitors are asked to leave the castle before six o'clock

    v) It is used in the idiom **jemand (gut) leiden mögen**:

        ich mag ihn gut leiden
        I like him

d) müssen

    i) **müssen** is used to express necessity:

        ich muß schon sagen ...   **ich mußte mich beeilen**
        I really must say ...   I had to hurry

    ii) It can also express supposition:

        jemand muß es versteckt haben
        someone must have hidden it

    iii) In the imperfect subjunctive it expresses a wish or hope:

        das müßte eigentlich passen   **Geld müßte man haben!**
        that ought to fit   it would be nice to have money

    iv) The negative of **müssen** is not the same as 'must not' in English:

        du mußt nicht kommen
        you don't have to come

        If you want to say 'you must not come' then German uses **dürfen**:

        du darfst nicht kommen
        you must not come

e) **sollen**

   i) **sollen** expresses duty or obligation:

   du sollst nicht töten **er sollte seinem Vater helfen**
   thou shalt not kill he ought to help his father

   ich hätte es früher tun sollen
   I ought to have done it earlier

Note: there is sometimes a distinction in this sense between the present and the imperfect subjunctive. The present tense implies that the obligation is imposed from outside, the imperfect subjunctive that it comes from within the speaker:

   ich soll nicht rauchen
   I shouldn't smoke (- *my doctor's told me*)

   ich sollte nicht rauchen
   I shouldn't smoke (- *I know it's bad for me*)

   ii) **sollen** is used to express a rumour or generally held opinion:

   dieser soll der beste sein
   this one is supposed to be the best

   es sollte heute regnen, hat aber nicht
   it was supposed to rain today but didn't

   iii) The imperfect tense of **sollen** can be used to express a future in the past:

   das sollte ihn teuer zu stehen kommen
   he was to pay dearly for it

   das sollten wir später erfahren
   we were to find that out later

f) **wollen**

   i) **wollen** expresses intention or desire:

   er will nur dein Bestes **ich will sie heiraten**
   he only wants the best for you I'm determined to marry her

   Note the use with non-personal subjects in the sense of 'to refuse to':

   der Regen wollte nicht enden
   the rain just wouldn't stop

   der Motor wollte nicht anspringen
   the engine refused to start

Note the construction with **daß**:

alle wollen, daß du kommst
everyone wants you to come

er will, daß ich ihm helfe
he wants me to help him

ii) **wollen** is used to express a claim made by someone and reported by the speaker:

er will das Geld gar nicht gesehen haben
he claims he never saw the money

er will alles besser wissen
he always thinks he knows best

iii) In the imperfect tense and followed by **gerade** it is the equivalent of 'to be about to':

er wollte gerade verschwinden
he was about to disappear

iv) **wollen** is used with the passive infinitive in the sense of 'must':

der Fall will vorsichtig behandelt werden
the case must be handled carefully

g) *the omission of the infinitive with the modal*

Infinitives expressing movement may be omitted when it is clear what is intended; this is usually when there is an adverb or adverbial phrase expressing direction:

du sollst sofort in die Schule
you are to go to school at once

ich muß heute nach Dortmund
I have to go to Dortmund today

ich darf nicht nach draußen
I'm not allowed out

The alternative perfect and pluperfect forms of the modal verbs often have different meanings.

er hat es tun sollen
he was supposed to do it

er soll es getan haben
he is supposed to have done it

er hat es tun müssen
he had to do it

er muß es getan haben
he must have done it

With **können** the distinction is less obvious from the English:

er hat es tun können
he could have done it (– *had the opportunity*)

er kann es getan haben
he may have done it (= *is a possible culprit*)
er hätte es tun können
he could have done it (= *if he had been willing*)
er könnte es getan haben
he might have done it (= *is a possible culprit*)

12. Impersonal verbs

a) Impersonal verbs are verbs which have **es** as subject when **es** does not refer to any specific person, thing or action. *Compare*:

    es ist besser zu gehen
    it's better to go (*impersonal*)

and: **dieses Buch?**   **es ist mein Lieblingsbuch**
this book?   it's my favourite ('*personal*', **es** *refers to the book*)

Impersonal verbs can be divided into two groups, depending on whether the **es** is kept when the subject and verb are inverted:

    es gibt kein Essen heute   >   **heute gibt's kein Essen**
    there's no food today

    es ist mir kalt   >   **mir ist kalt**
    I'm cold

b) Apart from those listed under c) below, impersonal verbs and expressions retain the **es** in inversion. In some cases the **es** in inversion is optional. Below are some of the main types of impersonal verbs that keep the **es**:

Verbs of weather and similar phenomena:

es regnet	it is raining
es schneit	it is snowing
es hagelt	it is hailing
es blitzt	there is lightning
es donnert	there is thunder
es dunkelt	it's getting dark
es friert	it is freezing
es tagt	it's getting light
es dämmert	dawn/twilight is coming
es wird Sommer	summer is coming
es brennt	there's a fire
es zieht	there's a draught
es geistert	there are ghosts about

Note: some of these may be used to refer to persons:

es friert mich	**es ist mir kalt**
I'm freezing	I'm cold

This form is felt to be slightly stilted and inversion is common:

mich friert (es)	**mir ist (es) kalt**

The **es** may be kept but is usually omitted.

Verbs of noise:

es klingelt	there's a ring
es klopft	there's a knock
es läutet	there's a ring
es raschelt	there's a rustling

Other impersonal verbs:

es gefällt mir	I like it
es geht	it's all right
es gibt	there is
es handelt sich um	it is a matter of
es kommt darauf an	it depends

Note: **es war einmal** ('once upon a time') is never inverted

c) Impersonal verbs where **es** is omitted in inversion

In expressions formed with **es ist** + adjectives expressing a state of mind, body or health the **es** is normally omitted in inversion:

ihm war traurig zumute	he felt sad
mir ist warm	I feel warm
mir wird besser	I'm getting better
ihr ist schlecht	she feels sick

In the impersonal passive the **es** is always omitted in inversion:

die ganze Nacht hindurch wurde getanzt
the dancing went on all night

ihm wurde der Preis verliehen
he was awarded the prize

Verbs indicating position omit the **es** in inversion; the commonest are **liegen**, **sein** and **stehen**:

es steht in der Zeitung, daß ... > in der Zeitung steht, daß ...
it says in the paper that ...

VERBS

d) *es gibt* or *es ist?*

es gibt is the usual German translation for 'there is/are'; the verb is always in the singular:

gibt es einen Aufzug? **es gibt nie Ruhe hier**
is there a lift? there's never any peace and quiet here

zum Abendessen gibt es Forellen
there is trout for dinner

es ist/sind is only used when there is an indication of place or position. *Compare*:

es ist Post da *and:* **heute gibt es keine Post**
the post has arrived there's no post today

es ist/sind is particulary common when the presence is only temporary:

es sind zwei Mädchen an der Tur
there are two girls at the door

Note: **es ist/sind** loses the **es** in inversion:

in München war eine Demonstration
there was a demonstration in Munich

es ist/sind can be used for weather, but **es gibt** is also possible:

es gab diesen Sommer wenig Sonne
es hat diesen Sommer wenig Sonne gegeben
there wasn't much sun this summer

13. Reflexive verbs

a) Reflexive verbs are verbs used with a reflexive pronoun which relates the action back to the subject:

I washed myself: 'myself' is the reflexive pronoun.

b) German has both accusative and dative reflexive pronouns:

PERSON	ACCUSATIVE	DATIVE
ich	mich	mir
du	dich	dir
er/sie/es	sich	sich
wir	uns	uns
ihr	euch	euch
Sie/sie	sich	sich

160 VERBS

There are some German verbs which only occur as reflexives and the English equivalent to which contains no reflexive pronoun:

beeil dich!   **ich habe mich dazu entschlossen**
hurry up   I have decided to do it

c) The position of the reflexive pronoun

The reflexive pronoun usually comes immediately after the verb:

mein Vater erinnert sich daran
my father remembers it

With inversion or when the finite verb is at the end it usually follows a pronoun subject but comes before other pronouns:

erinnert sich dein Vater daran?
does your father remember it?

erinnert er sich daran?   **erinnert sich einer daran?**
does he remember it?   does anyone remember it?

In an infinitive phrase the reflexive pronoun comes first:

ich darf nicht vergessen, mir ein neues Taschentuch zu kaufen
I mustn't forget to buy a new handkerchief

The reflexive cannot precede the finite verb in normal word order.

Note: All reflexive verbs form their perfect tense with **haben**. The conjugation is as for other verbs.

d) Usage

The basic use is to relate the action of the verb back to the subject:

ich wasche mich   **du schadest dir dabei bloß selbst**
I wash myself   you'll only harm yourself

In the plural the relexive pronoun can be reciprocal and is often translated into English by 'each other':

wir sehen uns morgen
we'll see each other tomorrrow

This can also be expressed by **einander**:

sie sehen einander jeden Tag
they see each other every day

The accusative reflexive pronoun is used with many verbs with the prefix **ver-** to say that the action of the verb has been done wrongly:

ich habe mich versprochen
I made a slip of the tongue

er hat sich verzählt
he miscounted

e) There is an impersonal reflexive construction which expresses in general whether an activity is pleasant or easy or not:

in Turnschuhen läuft es sich bequem
trainers are comfortable to run in

in einem weichen Bett schläft es sich schlecht
soft beds are bad for sleeping in

With the reflexive form of **lassen** the verb following has a passive sense:

das läßt sich leicht machen
that's easily done

The dative reflexive can be used to indicate that the object belongs to the subject of the verb:

ich wasche mir die Hände
I wash my hands

sie zog sich die Schuhe an
she put her shoes on

The dative reflexive is also used with many verbs to emphasise the subject's interest or involvement in the activity of the verb. In these cases is it usual but not obligatory:

den Film sehe ich mir bestimmt an
I'm certainly going to see that film

du solltest dir einen neuen Wagen kaufen
you should buy a new car

When a pronoun used with a preposition refers back to the subject the reflexive pronoun must be used. (It is only in the **er/sie/es** and **sie** forms that it is actually different from the regular pronoun):

vor sich sah er jemand laufen
he saw someone running in front of him(self)

er sah jemand hinter ihm
he saw someone behind him (– *'him' not the same person as 'he'*)

14. Verbs taking the dative

a) The dative is used for the indirect object and comes after many verbs of giving, sending, telling. Often the fact that the object is in the dative will be clear from the English equivalent:

    bring mir die Teller!
    bring the plates to me

But: English often omits the 'to' as in: 'bring me the plates'.

German usage is sometimes different from English:

sagen Sie es mir!	**Sie wollten mich sprechen?**
tell me	you wanted to speak to me?

b) Many verbs take both a dative and an accusative object:

    er hat mir alles erzählt
    he told me everything

c) Verbs formed with the prefixes **bei-** and **nach-** and inseparable verbs with the prefix **ent-** with the basic meaning of 'to escape from' take the dative:

beistehen	to support
nachgeben	to give in to
entkommen	to escape from

d) Here is a list of many of the more common verbs that take a dative object. Verbs that fit into the categories above have largely been omitted:

auffallen	to strike, be noticed
ausweichen	to get out of the way of
befehlen	to order
begegnen	to meet
danken	to thank
dienen	to serve
empfehlen	to recommend
erlauben	to allow
fehlen	to be lacking
folgen	to follow
gefallen	to please
gehorchen	to obey
gehören	to belong to
gelingen	to succeed
genügen	to be enough for

glauben	to believe
gratulieren	to congratulate
helfen	to help
mißtrauen	to distrust
passen	to suit
raten	to advise
reichen	to be enough for
schaden	to harm
schmeicheln	to flatter
trauen	to trust
verbieten	to forbid
versichern	to assure
vertrauen	to trust
verzeihen	to forgive
vorstehen	to preside over
wehtun	to hurt
widersprechen	to contradict
widerstehen	to resist
zusehen	to watch
zustimmen	to agree to

15. Verbs with two accusative objects

A few verbs can be followed by two objects in the accusative. This is almost entirely restricted to **kosten** ('to cost'), **lehren** ('to teach'), **nennen** ('to call') and **fragen** ('to ask'):

das kann ihn den Kragen kosten
that might be his downfall

er nannte mich einen Dummkopf
he called me a fool

sie haben mich Schwieriges gefragt
they asked me difficult things

16. Verbs followed by prepositions

a) Many German verbs are followed by prepositions. Very often these are not the obvious ones from the English equivalent and should be learnt — along with the case if necessary — with the verb:

ich fürchte mich vor ihm
I'm afraid of him

Some verbs can be followed by different prepositions, usually with a change of meaning:

ich freue mich auf die Ferien
I'm looking forward to the holidays

sie hat sich über das Geschenk gefreut
she was pleased with the present

Such verbs often have a noun following the preposition. However, they can also be followed by an infinitive phrase or a subordinate clause — usually a **daß** clause. When they are followed by such an infinitive or clause it is very common to insert the preposition in the main clause with the prefix **da(r)-** before it:

ich erinnere mich an ihn
I remember him

ich erinnere mich daran, ihn gesehen zu haben
I remember seeing him

b) Here is a list of some of the more common verbs with prepositions:

i) **an** + *acc*
denken an	to think of (*have in one's mind*)
sich erinnern an	to remember
erinnern an	to remind
sich gewöhnen an	to become accustomed to

ii) **an** + *dat*
es fehlt an	there is a lack of
leiden an	to suffer from (*disease*)

iii) **auf** + *acc*
achtgeben auf	to pay attention to
aufpassen auf	to keep an eye on
sich beschränken auf	to restrict oneself to
sich freuen auf	to look forward to
hoffen auf	to hope for
reagieren auf	to react to
rechnen auf	to count on
sich verlassen auf	to rely upon
verzichten auf	to renounce
warten auf	to wait for

iv) **auf** + *dat*
bestehen auf	to insist upon

VERBS

- v) **aus** + *dat*
  - **bestehen aus** — consist of

- vi) **für** + *acc*
  - **sich bedanken für** — to say thank you for
  - **sich einsetzen für** — to do a lot for
  - **sich entscheiden für** — to decide in favour of
  - **halten für** — to consider
  - **sich interessieren für** — to be interested in
  - **sorgen für** — to look after

- vii) **mit** + *dat*
  - **aufhören mit** — to stop doing
  - **einverstanden sein mit** — to be in agreement with
  - **rechnen mit** — to count on

- viii) **nach** + *dat*
  - **fragen nach** — to ask for
  - **schmecken nach** — to taste of
  - **suchen nach** — to look for

- ix) **über** + *acc*
  - **sich freuen über** — to be pleased at
  - **lachen über** — to laugh at
  - **nachdenken über** — to reflect upon

- x) **um** + *acc*
  - **sich kümmern um** — to care for
  - **sich sorgen um** — to be worried about
  - **es geht um** — it is a matter of
  - **es handelt sich um** — it is a matter of

- xi) **unter** + *dat*
  - **leiden unter** — to suffer from (*noise etc*)
  - **verstehen unter** — to understand by

- xii) **von** + *dat*
  - **abhängen von** — to be dependent on
  - **sich erholen von** — to recuperate from
  - **handeln von** — to be about

- xiii) **vor** + *dat*
  - **sich fürchten vor** — to be afraid of

- xiv) **zu** + *dat*
  - **beitragen zu** — to contribute to
  - **sich entschließen zu** — to decide upon

17. List of irregular verbs

Notes: verbs with an asterisk (*) are conjugated with **sein**:

verbs with a prefix take the same forms as the simple verbs (without the prefix), eg **versprechen** and **aussprechen** take the same forms as **sprechen**;

past participles used after infinitives: **er hätte nicht bleiben wollen** (he wouldn't have wanted to stay)

Compare: **er hat nicht gewollt** (he didn't want to).

Infinitive	English	Present Indicative *3rd pers sing*	Imperfect Indicative	Past Participle
backen	to bake	bäckt, backt	backte	gebacken
befehlen	to order	befiehlt	befahl	befohlen
beginnen	to begin	beginnt	begann	begonnen
beißen	to bite	beißt	biß	gebissen
bergen	to salvage, rescue	birgt	barg	geborgen
bersten	to burst	birst	barst	geborsten*
bewegen	to persuade	bewegt	bewog	bewogen
biegen	to bend, turn	biegt	bog	gebogen
bieten	to offer	bietet	bot	geboten
binden	to tie	bindet	band	gebunden
bitten	to ask	bittet	bat	gebeten
blasen	to blow	bläst	blies	geblasen
bleiben	to stay	bleibt	blieb	geblieben*
braten	to fry	brät	briet	gebraten
brechen	to break	bricht	brach	gebrochen
brennen	to burn	brennt	brannte	gebrannt
bringen	to bring	bringt	brachte	gebracht
denken	to think	denkt	dachte	gedacht
dreschen	to thresh	drischt	drosch	gedroschen
dringen	to penetrate, urge	dringt	drang	gedrungen*
dürfen	to be allowed to	darf	durfte	gedurft; *(after infinitive)* dürfen
empfangen	to receive	empfängt	empfing	empfangen
empfehlen	to recommend	empfiehlt	empfahl	empfohlen
empfinden	to feel	empfindet	empfand	empfunden

VERBS

erschrecken	to be startled	erschreckt	erschrak	erschrocken*
essen	to eat	ißt	aß	gegessen
fahren	to drive	fährt	fuhr	gefahren*
fallen	to fall	fällt	fiel	gefallen*
fangen	to catch	fängt	fing	gefangen
fechten	to fence	ficht	focht	gefochten
finden	to find	findet	fand	gefunden
flechten	to weave, twine	flicht	flocht	geflochten
fliegen	to fly	fliegt	flog	geflogen*
fliehen	to flee	flieht	floh	geflohen*
fließen	to flow	fließt	floß	geflossen*
fressen	to eat	frißt	fraß	gefressen
frieren	to freeze	friert	fror	gefroren
gebären	to give birth (to)	gebiert	gebar	geboren
geben	to give	gibt	gab	gegeben
gedeihen	to thrive	gedeiht	gedieh	gediehen*
gehen	to go	geht	ging	gegangen*
gelingen	to succeed	gelingt	gelang	gelungen*
gelten	to be valid	gilt	galt	gegolten
genesen	to recover, convalesce	genest	genas	genesen*
genießen	to enjoy	genießt	genoß	genossen
geschehen	to happen	geschieht	geschah	geschehen*
gewinnen	to win	gewinnt	gewann	gewonnen
gießen	to pour	gießt	goß	gegossen
gleichen	to resemble, be like	gleicht	glich	geglichen
gleiten	to glide	gleitet	glitt	geglitten*
glimmen	to glow	glimmt	glomm	geglommen
graben	to dig	gräbt	grub	gegraben
greifen	to grasp	greift	griff	gegriffen
haben	to have	hat	hatte	gehabt
halten	to hold	hält	hielt	gehalten
hängen	to hang	hängt	hing	gehangen
hauen	to hit, hew	haut	haute	gehauen
heben	to lift	hebt	hob	gehoben
heißen	to be called	heißt	hieß	geheißen
helfen	to help	hilft	half	geholfen
kennen	to know	kennt	kannte	gekannt
klingen	to sound	klingt	klang	geklungen
kneifen	to pinch	kneift	kniff	gekniffen
kommen	to come	kommt	kam	gekommen*
können	to be able to	kann	konnte	gekonnt; (after infinitive) können

168 VERBS

kriechen	to crawl	kriecht	kroch	gekrochen*
laden	to load	lädt	lud	geladen
lassen	to leave, let	läßt	ließ	gelassen; (after infinitive) lassen
laufen	to run	läuft	lief	gelaufen*
leiden	to suffer	leidet	litt	gelitten
leihen	to lend, borrow	leiht	lieh	geliehen
lesen	to read	liest	las	gelesen
liegen	to lie	liegt	lag	gelegen
lügen	to tell lies	lügt	log	gelogen
mahlen	to grind	mahlt	mahlte	gemahlen
meiden	to avoid	meidet	mied	gemieden
melken	to milk	melkt	melkte	gemolken
messen	to measure	mißt	maß	gemessen
mißlingen	to fail	mißlingt	mißlang	mißlungen*
mögen	to like	mag	mochte	gemocht; (after infinitive) mögen
müssen	to have to	muß	mußte	gemußt; (after infinitive) müssen
nehmen	to take	nimmt	nahm	genommen
nennen	to call, name	nennt	nannte	genannt
pfeifen	to whistle	pfeift	pfiff	gepfiffen
preisen	to praise	preist	pries	gepriesen
quellen	to pour	quillt	quoll	gequollen*
raten	to guess, advise	rät	riet	geraten
reiben	to rub	reibt	rieb	gerieben
reißen	to rip	reißt	riß	gerissen
reiten	to ride	reitet	ritt	geritten
rennen	to run	rennt	rannte	gerannt*
riechen	to smell	riecht	roch	gerochen
ringen	to wrestle, struggle	ringt	rang	gerungen
rinnen	to run (liquid)	rinnt	rann	geronnen*
rufen	to call	ruft	rief	gerufen
salzen	to salt	salzt	salzte	gesalzen
saufen	to drink	säuft	soff	gesoffen
saugen	to suck	saugt	sog, saugte	gesogen, gesaugt
schaffen	to create	schafft	schuf	geschaffen
scheiden	to separate	scheidet	schied	geschieden
scheinen	to shine, seem	scheint	schien	geschienen

VERBS 169

scheißen	to shit	scheißt	schiß	geschissen
schelten	to scold	schilt	schalt	gescholten
scheren	to shear	schert	schor	geschoren
schieben	to push	schiebt	schob	geschoben
schießen	to shoot	schießt	schoß	geschossen
schinden	to maltreat	schindet	schindete	geschunden
schlafen	to sleep	schläft	schlief	geschlafen
schlagen	to beat, hit	schlägt	schlug	geschlagen
schleichen	to creep	schleicht	schlich	geschlichen*
schleifen	to sharpen	schleift	schliff	geschliffen
schließen	to shut	schließt	schloß	geschlossen
schlingen	to tie	schlingt	schlang	geschlungen
schmeißen	to chuck	schmeißt	schmiß	geschmissen
schmelzen	to melt	schmilzt	schmolz	geschmolzen
schneiden	to cut	schneidet	schnitt	geschnitten
schreiben	to write	schreibt	schrieb	geschrieben
schreien	to shout	schreit	schrie	geschrie(e)n
schreiten	to stride	schreitet	schritt	geschritten*
schweigen	to be silent	schweigt	schwieg	geschwiegen
schwellen	to swell	schwillt	schwoll	geschwollen*
schwimmen	to swim	schwimmt	schwamm	geschwommen*
schwinden	to fade, dwindle	schwindet	schwand	geschwunden*
schwingen	to swing	schwingt	schwang	geschwungen
schwören	to swear	schwört	schwor	geschworen
sehen	to see	sieht	sah	gesehen; (after infinitive) sehen
sein	to be	ist	war	gewesen*
senden	to send	sendet	sandte	gesandt
singen	to sing	singt	sang	gesungen
sinken	to sink	sinkt	sank	gesunken*
sinnen	to ponder	sinnt	sann	gesonnen
sitzen	to sit	sitzt	saß	gesessen
sollen	to be supposed to	soll	sollte	gesollt; (after infinitive) sollen
spalten	to split	spaltet	spaltete	gespalten, gespaltet
speien	to spit, spew	speit	spie	gespie(e)n
spinnen	to spin	spinnt	spann	gesponnen
sprechen	to speak	spricht	sprach	gesprochen
sprießen	to sprout	sprießt	sproß, sprießte	gesprossen*
springen	to jump	springt	sprang	gesprungen*
stechen	to sting	sticht	stach	gestochen

170 VERBS

stecken	to be stuck	steckt	steckte, stak	gesteckt
stehen	to stand	steht	stand	gestanden
stehlen	to steal	stiehlt	stahl	gestohlen
steigen	to climb	steigt	stieg	gestiegen*
sterben	to die	stirbt	starb	gestorben*
stinken	to stink	stinkt	stank	gestunken
stoßen	to push	stößt	stieß	gestoßen
streichen	to paint, spread, stroke, delete	streicht	strich	gestrichen
streiten	to argue	streitet	stritt	gestritten
tragen	to carry, wear	trägt	trug	getragen
treffen	to meet, hit	trifft	traf	getroffen
treiben	to drive, float	treibt	trieb	getrieben
treten	to kick, tread	tritt	trat	getreten
trinken	to drink	trinkt	trank	getrunken
trügen	to deceive	trügt	trog	getrogen
tun	to do	tut	tat	getan
verderben	to spoil	verdirbt	verdarb	verdorben
verdrießen	to annoy	verdrießt	verdroß	verdrossen
vergessen	to forget	vergißt	vergaß	vergessen
verlieren	to lose	verliert	verlor	verloren
verschleißen	to wear out	verschleißt	verschliß	verschlissen
verzeihen	to forgive	verzeiht	verzieh	verziehen
wachsen	to grow	wächst	wuchs	gewachsen*
waschen	to wash	wäscht	wusch	gewaschen
weben	to weave	webt	webte, wob	gewebt, gewoben
weichen	to yield	weicht	wich	gewichen*
weisen	to show	weist	wies	gewiesen
wenden	to turn	wendet	wendete, wandte	gewendet, gewandt
werben	to advertise, recruit	wirbt	warb	geworben
werden	to become	wird	wurde	geworden*; (after past participle) worden
werfen	to throw	wirft	warf	geworfen
wiegen	to weigh	wiegt	wog	gewogen
winden	to wind	windet	wand	gewunden
winken	to wave	winkt	winkte	gewinkt, gewunken
wissen	to know	weiß	wußte	gewußt

wollen	*to want to*	will	wollte	gewollt; (*after infinitive*) wollen
wringen	*to wring*	wringt	wrang	gewrungen
ziehen	*to pull*	zieht	zog	gezogen
zwingen	*to force*	zwingt	zwang	gezwungen

172 VERBS

D. CONJUGATION TABLES

The following verbs provide the main patterns of conjugation including the conjugation of some common irregular verbs. They are arranged in alphabetical order.

Verb with auxiliary **haben** (*see p 131-2*)	BRAUCHEN
Verb with auxiliary **sein** (*see p 132-3*)	STÜRZEN
Reflexive verb (*see p 159-61*)	SICH BEEILEN
Separable verb (*see p 135-6*)	ABLEHNEN
Auxiliaries (*see p 10*)	HABEN SEIN WERDEN

Verbs with special endings (*see p 112*)
  Verb in **-den/-ten/-men/-nen**
  Verb in **-ln/-rn**
  Verb in **-ssen**
	
	WARTEN
	ÄRGERN
	PASSEN

Modal verbs (*see p 124-8, 152-7*)	DÜRFEN KÖNNEN MÖGEN MÜSSEN SOLLEN WOLLEN

'Harrap's German Verbs', a fully comprehensive list of German verbs and their conjugations, is also available in this series.

ABLEHNEN to reject, decline

PRESENT	**IMPERFECT**	**FUTURE**
ich lehne ab	ich lehnte ab	ich werde ablehnen
du lehnst ab	du lehntest ab	du wirst ablehnen
er/sie lehnt ab	er/sie lehnte ab	er/sie wird ablehnen
wir lehnen ab	wir lehnten ab	wir werden ablehnen
ihr lehnt ab	ihr lehntet ab	ihr werdet ablehnen
Sie lehnen ab	Sie lehnten ab	Sie werden ablehnen
sie lehnen ab	sie lehnten ab	sie werden ablehnen

PERFECT	**PLUPERFECT**	**CONDITIONAL**
ich habe abgelehnt	ich hatte abgelehnt	ich würde ablehnen
du hast abgelehnt	du hattest abgelehnt	du würdest ablehnen
er/sie hat abgelehnt	er/sie hatte abgelehnt	er/sie würde ablehnen
wir haben abgelehnt	wir hatten abgelehnt	wir würden ablehnen
ihr habt abgelehnt	ihr hattet abgelehnt	ihr würdet ablehnen
Sie haben abgelehnt	Sie hatten abgelehnt	Sie würden ablehnen
sie haben abgelehnt	sie hatten abgelehnt	sie würden ablehnen

SUBJUNCTIVE

PRESENT	**PERFECT**
ich lehne ab	ich habe abgelehnt
du lehnest ab	du habest abgelehnt
er/sie lehne ab	er/sie habe abgelehnt
wir lehnen ab	wir haben abgelehnt
ihr lehnet ab	ihr habet abgelehnt
Sie lehnen ab	Sie haben abgelehnt
sie lehnen ab	sie haben abgelehnt

IMPERFECT	**PLUPERFECT**
ich lehnte ab	ich hätte abgelehnt
du lehntest ab	du hättest abgelehnt
er/sie lehnte ab	er/sie hätte abgelehnt
wir lehnten ab	wir hätten abgelehnt
ihr lehntet ab	ihr hättet abgelehnt
Sie lehnten ab	Sie hätten abgelehnt
sie lehnten ab	sie hätten abgelehnt

INFINITIVE
PRESENT
ablehnen
PAST
abgelehnt haben

PARTICIPLE
PRESENT
ablehnend
PAST
abgelehnt

IMPERATIVE
lehn(e) ab!
lehnt ab!
lehnen Sie ab!
lehnen wir ab!

FUTURE PERFECT
ich werde abgelehnt haben
du wirst abgelehnt haben *etc*

ÄRGERN to annoy

PRESENT	IMPERFECT	FUTURE
ich ärg(e)re	ich ärgerte	ich werde ärgern
du ärgerst	du ärgertest	du wirst ärgern
er/sie ärgert	er/sie ärgerte	er/sie wird ärgern
wir ärgern	wir ärgerten	wir werden ärgern
ihr ärgert	ihr ärgertet	ihr werdet ärgern
Sie ärgern	Sie ärgerten	Sie werden ärgern
sie ärgern	sie ärgerten	sie werden ärgern

PERFECT	PLUPERFECT	CONDITIONAL
ich habe geärgert	ich hatte geärgert	ich würde ärgern
du hast geärgert	du hattest geärgert	du würdest ärgern
er/sie hat geärgert	er/sie hatte geärgert	er/sie würde ärgern
wir haben geärgert	wir hatten geärgert	wir würden ärgern
ihr habt geärgert	ihr hattet geärgert	ihr würdet ärgern
Sie haben geärgert	Sie hatten geärgert	Sie würden ärgern
sie haben geärgert	sie hatten geärgert	sie würden ärgern

SUBJUNCTIVE

PRESENT	PERFECT
ich ärgere	ich habe geärgert
du ärgerest	du habest geärgert
er/sie ärgere	er/sie habe geärgert
wir ärgeren	wir haben geärgert
ihr ärgeret	ihr habet geärgert
Sie ärgeren	Sie haben geärgert
sie ärgeren	sie haben geärgert

IMPERFECT	PLUPERFECT
ich ärgerte	ich hätte geärgert
du ärgertest	du hättest geärgert
er/sie ärgerte	er/sie hätte geärgert
wir ärgerten	wir hätten geärgert
ihr ärgertet	ihr hättet geärgert
Sie ärgerten	Sie hätten geärgert
sie ärgerten	sie hätten geärgert

INFINITIVE
PRESENT
ärgern
PAST
geärgert haben

PARTICIPLE
PRESENT
ärgernd
PAST
geärgert

IMPERATIVE
ärg(e)re!
ärgert!
ärgern Sie!
ärgern wir!

FUTURE PERFECT
ich werde geärgert haben
du wirst geärgert haben *etc*

SICH BEEILEN to hurry, rush

PRESENT
ich beeile mich
du beeilst dich
er/sie beeilt sich
wir beeilen uns
ihr beeilt euch
Sie beeilen sich
sie beeilen sich

IMPERFECT
ich beeilte mich
du beeiltest dich
er/sie beeilte sich
wir beeilten uns
ihr beeiltet euch
Sie beeilten sich
sie beeilten sich

FUTURE
ich werde mich beeilen
du wirst dich beeilen
er/sie wird sich beeilen
wir werden uns beeilen
ihr werdet euch beeilen
Sie werden sich beeilen
sie werden sich beeilen

PERFECT
ich habe mich beeilt
du hast dich beeilt
er/sie hat sich beeilt
wir haben uns beeilt
ihr habt euch beeilt
Sie haben sich beeilt
sie haben sich beeilt

PLUPERFECT
ich hatte mich beeilt
du hattest dich beeilt
er/sie hatte sich beeilt
wir hatten uns beeilt
ihr hattet euch beeilt
Sie hatten sich beeilt
sie hatten sich beeilt

CONDITIONAL
ich würde mich beeilen
du würdest dich beeilen
er/sie würde sich beeilen
wir würden uns beeilen
ihr würdet euch beeilen
Sie würden sich beeilen
sie würden sich beeilen

SUBJUNCTIVE
PRESENT
ich beeile mich
du beeilest dich
er/sie beeile sich
wir beeilen uns
ihr beeilet euch
Sie beeilen sich
sie beeilen sich

PERFECT
ich habe mich beeilt
du habest dich beeilt
er/sie habe sich beeilt
wir haben uns beeilt
ihr habet euch beeilt
Sie haben sich beeilt
sie haben sich beeilt

INFINITIVE
PRESENT
sich beeilen

PAST
sich beeilt haben

PARTICIPLE
PRESENT
mich/sich *etc* beeilend

IMPERFECT
ich beeilte mich
du beeiltest dich
er/sie beeilte sich
wir beeilten uns
ihr beeiltet euch
Sie beeilten sich
sie beeilten sich

PLUPERFECT
ich hätte mich beeilt
du hättest dich beeilt
er/sie hätte sich beeilt
wir hätten uns beeilt
ihr hättet euch beeilt
Sie hätten sich beeilt
sie hätten sich beeilt

IMPERATIVE
beeile dich!
beeilt euch!
beeilen Sie sich!
beeilen wir uns!

FUTURE PERFECT
ich werde mich beeilt haben
du wirst dich beeilt haben *etc*

VERBS

BRAUCHEN to need

PRESENT	**IMPERFECT**	**FUTURE**
ich brauche	ich brauchte	ich werde brauchen
du brauchst	du brauchtest	du wirst brauchen
er/sie braucht	er/sie brauchte	er/sie wird brauchen
wir brauchen	wir brauchten	wir werden brauchen
ihr braucht	ihr brauchtet	ihr werdet brauchen
Sie brauchen	Sie brauchten	Sie werden brauchen
sie brauchen	sie brauchten	sie werden brauchen

PERFECT	**PLUPERFECT**	**CONDITIONAL**
ich habe gebraucht	ich hatte gebraucht	ich würde brauchen
du hast gebraucht	du hattest gebraucht	du würdest brauchen
er/sie hat gebraucht	er/sie hatte gebraucht	er/sie würde brauchen
wir haben gebraucht	wir hatten gebraucht	wir würden brauchen
ihr habt gebraucht	ihr hattet gebraucht	ihr würdet brauchen
Sie haben gebraucht	Sie hatten gebraucht	Sie würden brauchen
sie haben gebraucht	sie hatten gebraucht	sie würden brauchen

SUBJUNCTIVE

PRESENT	**PERFECT**
ich brauche	ich habe gebraucht
du brauchest	du habest gebraucht
er/sie brauche	er/sie habe gebraucht
wir brauchen	wir haben gebraucht
ihr brauchet	ihr habet gebraucht
Sie brauchen	Sie haben gebraucht
sie brauchen	sie haben gebraucht

IMPERFECT	**PLUPERFECT**
ich brauchte	ich hätte gebraucht
du brauchtest	du hättest gebraucht
er/sie brauchte	er/sie hätte gebraucht
wir brauchten	wir hätten gebraucht
ihr brauchtet	ihr hättet gebraucht
Sie brauchten	Sie hätten gebraucht
sie brauchten	sie hätten gebraucht

INFINITIVE
PRESENT
brauchen
PAST
gebraucht haben

PARTICIPLE
PRESENT
brauchend
PAST
gebraucht

IMPERATIVE
brauch(e)!
braucht!
brauchen Sie!
brauchen wir!

FUTURE PERFECT
ich werde gebraucht haben
du wirst gebraucht haben *etc*

VERBS 177

DÜRFEN to be allowed to

PRESENT	**IMPERFECT**	**FUTURE**
ich darf	ich durfte	ich werde dürfen
du darfst	du durftest	du wirst dürfen
er/sie darf	er/sie durfte	er/sie wird dürfen
wir dürfen	wir durften	wir werden dürfen
ihr dürft	ihr durftet	ihr werdet dürfen
Sie dürfen	Sie durften	Sie werden dürfen
sie dürfen	sie durften	sie werden dürfen

PERFECT *(1)*	**PLUPERFECT** *(2)*	**CONDITIONAL**
ich habe gedurft	ich hatte gedurft	ich würde dürfen
du hast gedurft	du hattest gedurft	du würdest dürfen
er/sie hat gedurft	er/sie hatte gedurft	er/sie würde dürfen
wir haben gedurft	wir hatten gedurft	wir würden dürfen
ihr habt gedurft	ihr hattet gedurft	ihr würdet dürfen
Sie haben gedurft	Sie hatten gedurft	Sie würden dürfen
sie haben gedurft	sie hatten gedurft	sie würden dürfen

SUBJUNCTIVE

PRESENT	**PERFECT** *(1)*
ich dürfe	ich habe gedurft
du dürfest	du habest gedurft
er/sie dürfe	er/sie habe gedurft
wir dürfen	wir haben gedurft
ihr dürfet	ihr habet gedurft
Sie dürfen	Sie haben gedurft
sie dürfen	sie haben gedurft

IMPERFECT	**PLUPERFECT** *(3)*
ich dürfte	ich hätte gedurft
du dürftest	du hättest gedurft
er/sie dürfte	er/sie hätte gedurft
wir dürften	wir hätten gedurft
ihr dürftet	ihr hättet gedurft
Sie dürften	Sie hätten gedurft
sie dürften	sie hätten gedurft

INFINITIVE
PRESENT
dürfen

PAST
gedurft haben

PARTICIPLE
PRESENT
dürfend

PAST
gedurft

NOTE *when preceded by an infinitive: (1) ich habe ... dürfen etc (2) ich hatte ... dürfen etc (3) ich hätte ... dürfen etc*

VERBS

HABEN to have

PRESENT	IMPERFECT	FUTURE
ich habe	ich hatte	ich werde haben
du hast	du hattest	du wirst haben
er/sie hat	er/sie hatte	er/sie wird haben
wir haben	wir hatten	wir werden haben
ihr habt	ihr hattet	ihr werdet haben
Sie haben	Sie hatten	Sie werden haben
sie haben	sie hatten	sie werden haben

PERFECT	PLUPERFECT	CONDITIONAL
ich habe gehabt	ich hatte gehabt	ich würde haben
du hast gehabt	du hattest gehabt	du würdest haben
er/sie hat gehabt	er/sie hatte gehabt	er/sie würde haben
wir haben gehabt	wir hatten gehabt	wir würden haben
ihr habt gehabt	ihr hattet gehabt	ihr würdet haben
Sie haben gehabt	Sie hatten gehabt	Sie würden haben
sie haben gehabt	sie hatten gehabt	sie würden haben

SUBJUNCTIVE

PRESENT	PERFECT
ich habe	ich habe gehabt
du habest	du habest gehabt
er/sie habe	er/sie habe gehabt
wir haben	wir haben gehabt
ihr habet	ihr habet gehabt
Sie haben	Sie haben gehabt
sie haben	sie haben gehabt

IMPERFECT	PLUPERFECT
ich hätte	ich hätte gehabt
du hättest	du hättest gehabt
er/sie hätte	er/sie hätte gehabt
wir hätten	wir hätten gehabt
ihr hättet	ihr hättet gehabt
Sie hätten	Sie hätten gehabt
sie hätten	sie hätten gehabt

INFINITIVE
PRESENT
haben
PAST
gehabt haben

PARTICIPLE
PRESENT
habend
PAST
gehabt

IMPERATIVE
hab(e)!
habt!
haben Sie!
haben wir!

FUTURE PERFECT
ich werde gehabt haben
du wirst gehabt haben *etc*

VERBS 179

KÖNNEN to be able to

PRESENT	IMPERFECT	FUTURE
ich kann	ich konnte	ich werde können
du kannst	du konntest	du wirst können
er/sie kann	er/sie konnte	er/sie wird können
wir können	wir konnten	wir werden können
ihr könnt	ihr konntet	ihr werdet können
Sie können	Sie konnten	Sie werden können
sie können	sie konnten	sie werden können

PERFECT (1)	PLUPERFECT (2)	CONDITIONAL
ich habe gekonnt	ich hatte gekonnt	ich würde können
du hast gekonnt	du hattest gekonnt	du würdest können
er/sie hat gekonnt	er/sie hatte gekonnt	er/sie würde können
wir haben gekonnt	wir hatten gekonnt	wir würden können
ihr habt gekonnt	ihr hattet gekonnt	ihr würdet können
Sie haben gekonnt	Sie hatten gekonnt	Sie würden können
sie haben gekonnt	sie hatten gekonnt	sie würden können

SUBJUNCTIVE

PRESENT	PERFECT (1)
ich könne	ich habe gekonnt
du könnest	du habest gekonnt
er/sie könne	er/sie habe gekonnt
wir können	wir haben gekonnt
ihr könnet	ihr habet gekonnt
Sie können	Sie haben gekonnt
sie können	sie haben gekonnt

INFINITIVE

PRESENT
können

PAST
gekonnt haben

PARTICIPLE

PRESENT
könnend

PAST
gekonnt

IMPERFECT	PLUPERFECT (3)
ich könnte	ich hätte gekonnt
du könntest	du hättest gekonnt
er/sie könnte	er/sie hätte gekonnt
wir könnten	wir hätten gekonnt
ihr könntet	ihr hättet gekonnt
Sie könnten	Sie hätten gekonnt
sie könnten	sie hätten gekonnt

NOTE *when preceded by an infinitive: (1) ich habe ... können etc (2) ich hatte ... können etc (3) ich hätte ... können etc*

MÖGEN to like

PRESENT	IMPERFECT	FUTURE
ich mag	ich mochte	ich werde mögen
du magst	du mochtest	du wirst mögen
er/sie mag	er/sie mochte	er/sie wird mögen
wir mögen	wir mochten	wir werden mögen
ihr mögt	ihr mochtet	ihr werdet mögen
Sie mögen	Sie mochten	Sie werden mögen
sie mögen	sie mochten	sie werden mögen

PERFECT (1)	PLUPERFECT (2)	CONDITIONAL
ich habe gemocht	ich hatte gemocht	ich würde mögen
du hast gemocht	du hattest gemocht	du würdest mögen
er/sie hat gemocht	er/sie hatte gemocht	er/sie würde mögen
wir haben gemocht	wir hatten gemocht	wir würden mögen
ihr habt gemocht	ihr hattet gemocht	ihr würdet mögen
Sie haben gemocht	Sie hatten gemocht	Sie würden mögen
sie haben gemocht	sie hatten gemocht	sie würden mögen

SUBJUNCTIVE

PRESENT	PERFECT (1)
ich möge	ich habe gemocht
du mögest	du habest gemocht
er/sie möge	er/sie habe gemocht
wir mögen	wir haben gemocht
ihr möget	ihr habet gemocht
Sie mögen	Sie haben gemocht
sie mögen	sie haben gemocht

IMPERFECT	PLUPERFECT (3)
ich möchte	ich hätte gemocht
du möchtest	du hättest gemocht
er/sie möchte	er/sie hätte gemocht
wir möchten	wir hätten gemocht
ihr möchtet	ihr hättet gemocht
Sie möchten	Sie hätten gemocht
sie möchten	sie hätten gemocht

INFINITIVE
PRESENT
mögen

PAST
gemocht haben

PARTICIPLE
PRESENT
mögend

PAST
gemocht

NOTE *when preceded by an infinitive:* (1) ich habe ... mögen *etc* (2) ich hatte ... mögen *etc* (3) ich hätte ... mögen *etc*

VERBS 181

MÜSSEN to have to

PRESENT
ich muß
du mußt
er/sie muß
wir müssen
ihr müßt
Sie müssen
sie müssen

IMPERFECT
ich mußte
du mußtest
er/sie mußte
wir mußten
ihr mußtet
Sie mußten
sie mußten

FUTURE
ich werde müssen
du wirst müssen
er/sie wird müssen
wir werden müssen
ihr werdet müssen
Sie werden müssen
sie werden müssen

PERFECT (1)
ich habe gemußt
du hast gemußt
er/sie hat gemußt
wir haben gemußt
ihr habt gemußt
Sie haben gemußt
sie haben gemußt

PLUPERFECT (2)
ich hatte gemußt
du hattest gemußt
er/sie hatte gemußt
wir hatten gemußt
ihr hattet gemußt
Sie hatten gemußt
sie hatten gemußt

CONDITIONAL
ich würde müssen
du würdest müssen
er/sie würde müssen
wir würden müssen
ihr würdet müssen
Sie würden müssen
sie würden müssen

SUBJUNCTIVE
PRESENT
ich müße
du müßest
er/sie müße
wir müssen
ihr müßet
Sie müssen
sie müssen

PERFECT (1)
ich habe gemußt
du habest gemußt
er/sie habe gemußt
wir haben gemußt
ihr habet gemußt
Sie haben gemußt
sie haben gemußt

INFINITIVE
PRESENT
müssen
PAST
gemußt haben

PARTICIPLE
PRESENT
müssend
PAST
gemußt

IMPERFECT
ich müßte
du müßtest
er/sie müßte
wir müßten
ihr müßtet
Sie müßten
sie müßten

PLUPERFECT (3)
ich hätte gemußt
du hättest gemußt
er/sie hätte gemußt
wir hätten gemußt
ihr hättet gemußt
Sie hätten gemußt
sie hätten gemußt

NOTE *when preceded by an infinitive: (1) ich habe ... müssen etc (2) ich hatte ... müssen etc (3) ich hätte ... müssen etc*

PASSEN to fit, suit

PRESENT	IMPERFECT	FUTURE
ich passe	ich paßte	ich werde passen
du paßt	du paßtest	du wirst passen
er/sie paßt	er/sie paßte	er/sie wird passen
wir passen	wir paßten	wir werden passen
ihr paßt	ihr paßtet	ihr werdet passen
Sie passen	Sie paßten	Sie werden passen
sie passen	sie paßten	sie werden passen

PERFECT	PLUPERFECT	CONDITIONAL
ich habe gepaßt	ich hatte gepaßt	ich würde passen
du hast gepaßt	du hattest gepaßt	du würdest passen
er/sie hat gepaßt	er/sie hatte gepaßt	er/sie würde passen
wir haben gepaßt	wir hatten gepaßt	wir würden passen
ihr habt gepaßt	ihr hattet gepaßt	ihr würdet passen
Sie haben gepaßt	Sie hatten gepaßt	Sie würden passen
sie haben gepaßt	sie hatten gepaßt	sie würden passen

SUBJUNCTIVE

PRESENT	PERFECT
ich passe	ich habe gepaßt
du passest	du habest gepaßt
er/sie passe	er/sie habe gepaßt
wir passen	wir haben gepaßt
ihr passet	ihr habet gepaßt
Sie passen	Sie haben gepaßt
sie passen	sie haben gepaßt

IMPERFECT	PLUPERFECT
ich paßte	ich hätte gepaßt
du paßtest	du hättest gepaßt
er/sie paßte	er/sie hätte gepaßt
wir paßten	wir hätten gepaßt
ihr paßtet	ihr hättet gepaßt
Sie paßten	Sie hätten gepaßt
sie paßten	sie hätten gepaßt

INFINITIVE
PRESENT
passen
PAST
gepaßt haben

PARTICIPLE
PRESENT
passend
PAST
gepaßt

IMPERATIVE
paß! passe!
paßt!
passen Sie!
passen wir!

FUTURE PERFECT
ich werde gepaßt haben
du wirst gepaßt haben *etc*

SEIN to be

PRESENT	**IMPERFECT**	**FUTURE**
ich bin	ich war	ich werde sein
du bist	du warst	du wirst sein
er/sie ist	er/sie war	er/sie wird sein
wir sind	wir waren	wir werden sein
ihr seid	ihr wart	ihr werdet sein
Sie sind	Sie waren	Sie werden sein
sie sind	sie waren	sie werden sein

PERFECT	**PLUPERFECT**	**CONDITIONAL**
ich bin gewesen	ich war gewesen	ich würde sein
du bist gewesen	du warst gewesen	du würdest sein
er/sie ist gewesen	er/sie war gewesen	er/sie würde sein
wir sind gewesen	wir waren gewesen	wir würden sein
ihr seid gewesen	ihr wart gewesen	ihr würdet sein
Sie sind gewesen	Sie waren gewesen	Sie würden sein
sie sind gewesen	sie waren gewesen	sie würden sein

SUBJUNCTIVE

PRESENT	**PERFECT**
ich sei	ich sei gewesen
du sei(e)st	du sei(e)st gewesen
er/sie sei	er/sie sei gewesen
wir seien	wir seien gewesen
ihr seiet	ihr seiet gewesen
Sie seien	Sie seien gewesen
sie seien	sie seien gewesen

IMPERFECT	**PLUPERFECT**
ich wäre	ich wäre gewesen
du wär(e)st	du wär(e)st gewesen
er/sie wäre	er/sie wäre gewesen
wir wären	wir wären gewesen
ihr wär(e)t	ihr wär(e)t gewesen
Sie wären	Sie wären gewesen
sie wären	sie wären gewesen

INFINITIVE
PRESENT
sein
PAST
gewesen sein

PARTICIPLE
PRESENT
seiend
PAST
gewesen

IMPERATIVE
sei!
seid!
seien Sie!
seien wir!

FUTURE PERFECT
ich werde gewesen sein
du wirst gewesen sein *etc*

184 VERBS

SOLLEN to be supposed to

PRESENT	IMPERFECT	FUTURE
ich soll	ich sollte	ich werde sollen
du sollst	du solltest	du wirst sollen
er/sie soll	er/sie sollte	er/sie wird sollen
wir sollen	wir sollten	wir werden sollen
ihr sollt	ihr solltet	ihr werdet sollen
Sie sollen	Sie sollten	Sie werden sollen
sie sollen	sie sollten	sie werden sollen

PERFECT (1)	PLUPERFECT (2)	CONDITIONAL
ich habe gesollt	ich hatte gesollt	ich würde sollen
du hast gesollt	du hattest gesollt	du würdest sollen
er/sie hat gesollt	er/sie hatte gesollt	er/sie würde sollen
wir haben gesollt	wir hatten gesollt	wir würden sollen
ihr habt gesollt	ihr hattet gesollt	ihr würdet sollen
Sie haben gesollt	Sie hatten gesollt	Sie würden sollen
sie haben gesollt	sie hatten gesollt	sie würden sollen

SUBJUNCTIVE

PRESENT	PERFECT (1)
ich solle	ich habe gesollt
du sollest	du habest gesollt
er/sie solle	er/sie habe gesollt
wir sollen	wir haben gesollt
ihr sollet	ihr habet gesollt
Sie sollen	Sie haben gesollt
sie sollen	sie haben gesollt

INFINITIVE
PRESENT
sollen
PAST
gesollt haben

PARTICIPLE
PRESENT
sollend
PAST
gesollt

IMPERATIVE

IMPERFECT	PLUPERFECT (3)
ich sollte	ich hätte gesollt
du solltest	du hättest gesollt
er/sie sollte	er/sie hätte gesollt
wir sollten	wir hätten gesollt
ihr solltet	ihr hättet gesollt
Sie sollten	Sie hätten gesollt
sie sollten	sie hätten gesollt

NOTE when preceded by an infinitive: (1) ich habe ... sollen etc (2) ich hatte ... sollen etc (3) ich hätte ... sollen etc

STÜRZEN to drop

PRESENT	IMPERFECT	FUTURE
ich stürze	ich stürzte	ich werde stürzen
du stürzst	du stürztest	du wirst stürzen
er/sie stürzt	er/sie stürzte	er/sie wird stürzen
wir stürzen	wir stürzten	wir werden stürzen
ihr stürzt	ihr stürztet	ihr werdet stürzen
Sie stürzen	Sie stürzten	Sie werden stürzen
sie stürzen	sie stürzten	sie werden stürzen

PERFECT	PLUPERFECT	CONDITIONAL
ich bin gestürzt	ich war gestürzt	ich würde stürzen
du bist gestürzt	du warst gestürzt	du würdest stürzen
er/sie ist gestürzt	er/sie war gestürzt	er/sie würde stürzen
wir sind gestürzt	wir waren gestürzt	wir würden stürzen
ihr seid gestürzt	ihr wart gestürzt	ihr würdet stürzen
Sie sind gestürzt	Sie waren gestürzt	Sie würden stürzen
sie sind gestürzt	sie waren gestürzt	sie würden stürzen

SUBJUNCTIVE

PRESENT	PERFECT
ich stürze	ich sei gestürzt
du stürzest	du sei(e)st gestürzt
er/sie stürze	er/sie sei gestürzt
wir stürzen	wir seien gestürzt
ihr stürzet	ihr seiet gestürzt
Sie stürzen	Sie seien gestürzt
sie stürzen	sie seien gestürzt

IMPERFECT	PLUPERFECT
ich stürzte	ich wäre gestürzt
du stürztest	du wär(e)st gestürzt
er/sie stürzte	er/sie wäre gestürzt
wir stürzten	wir wären gestürzt
ihr stürztet	ihr wär(e)t gestürzt
Sie stürzten	Sie wären gestürzt
sie stürzten	sie wären gestürzt

INFINITIVE
PRESENT
stürzen
PAST
gestürzt sein

PARTICIPLE
PRESENT
stürzend
PAST
gestürzt

IMPERATIVE
stürz(e)!
stürzt!
stürzen Sie!
stürzen wir!

FUTURE PERFECT
ich werde gestürzt sein
du wirst gestürzt sein *etc*

VERBS

WARTEN to wait

PRESENT	IMPERFECT	FUTURE
ich warte	ich wartete	ich werde warten
du wartest	du wartetest	du wirst warten
er/sie wartet	er/sie wartete	er/sie wird warten
wir warten	wir warteten	wir werden warten
ihr wartet	ihr wartetet	ihr werdet warten
Sie warten	Sie warteten	Sie werden warten
sie warten	sie warteten	sie werden warten

PERFECT	PLUPERFECT	CONDITIONAL
ich habe gewartet	ich hatte gewartet	ich würde warten
du hast gewartet	du hattest gewartet	du würdest warten
er/sie hat gewartet	er/sie hatte gewartet	er/sie würde warten
wir haben gewartet	wir hatten gewartet	wir würden warten
ihr habt gewartet	ihr hattet gewartet	ihr würdet warten
Sie haben gewartet	Sie hatten gewartet	Sie würden warten
sie haben gewartet	sie hatten gewartet	sie würden warten

SUBJUNCTIVE

PRESENT	PERFECT
ich warte	ich habe gewartet
du wartest	du habest gewartet
er/sie warte	er/sie habe gewartet
wir warten	wir haben gewartet
ihr wartet	ihr habet gewartet
Sie warten	Sie haben gewartet
sie warten	sie haben gewartet

IMPERFECT	PLUPERFECT
ich wartete	ich hätte gewartet
du wartetest	du hättest gewartet
er/sie wartete	er/sie hätte gewartet
wir warteten	wir hätten gewartet
ihr wartetet	ihr hättet gewartet
Sie warteten	Sie hätten gewartet
sie warteten	sie hätten gewartet

INFINITIVE
PRESENT
warten
PAST
gewartet haben

PARTICIPLE
PRESENT
wartend
PAST
gewartet

IMPERATIVE
warte(e)!
wartet!
warten Sie!
warten wir!

FUTURE PERFECT
ich werde gewartet haben
du wirst gewartet haben *etc*

VERBS 187

WERDEN to become

PRESENT	**IMPERFECT**	**FUTURE**
ich werde	ich wurde	ich werde werden
du wirst	du wurdest	du wirst werden
er/sie wird	er/sie wurde	er/sie wird werden
wir werden	wir wurden	wir werden werden
ihr werdet	ihr wurdet	ihr werdet werden
Sie werden	Sie wurden	Sie werden werden
sie werden	sie wurden	sie werden werden

PERFECT (1)	**PLUPERFECT** (1)	**CONDITIONAL**
ich bin geworden	ich war geworden	ich würde werden
du bist geworden	du warst geworden	du würdest werden
er/sie ist geworden	er/sie war geworden	er/sie würde werden
wir sind geworden	wir waren geworden	wir würden werden
ihr seid geworden	ihr wart geworden	ihr würdet werden
Sie sind geworden	Sie waren geworden	Sie würden werden
sie sind geworden	sie waren geworden	sie würden werden

SUBJUNCTIVE

PRESENT	**PERFECT** (1)
ich werde	ich sei geworden
du werdest	du sei(e)st geworden
er/sie werde	er/sie sei geworden
wir werden	wir seien geworden
ihr werdet	ihr seiet geworden
Sie werden	Sie seien geworden
sie werden	sie seien geworden

INFINITIVE
PRESENT
werden
PAST (1)
geworden sein

PARTICIPLE
PRESENT
werdend
PAST
geworden

IMPERFECT	**PLUPERFECT** (1)
ich würde	ich wäre geworden
du würdest	du wär(e)st geworden
er/sie würde	er/sie wäre geworden
wir würden	wir wären geworden
ihr würdet	ihr wär(e)t geworden
Sie würden	Sie wären geworden
sie würden	sie wären geworden

IMPERATIVE
werde!
werdet!
werden Sie!
werden wir!

FUTURE PERFECT (1)
ich werde geworden sein
du wirst geworden sein *etc*

NOTE (1) geworden *becomes* worden *when preceded by a past participle to form the passive*

188 VERBS

WOLLEN to want (to)

PRESENT	IMPERFECT	FUTURE
ich will	ich wollte	ich werde wollen
du willst	du wolltest	du wirst wollen
er/sie will	er/sie wollte	er/sie wird wollen
wir wollen	wir wollten	wir werden wollen
ihr wollt	ihr wolltet	ihr werdet wollen
Sie wollen	Sie wollten	Sie werden wollen
sie wollen	sie wollten	sie werden wollen

PERFECT (1)	PLUPERFECT (2)	CONDITIONAL
ich habe gewollt	ich hatte gewollt	ich würde wollen
du hast gewollt	du hattest gewollt	du würdest wollen
er/sie hat gewollt	er/sie hatte gewollt	er/sie würde wollen
wir haben gewollt	wir hatten gewollt	wir würden wollen
ihr habt gewollt	ihr hattet gewollt	ihr würdet wollen
Sie haben gewollt	Sie hatten gewollt	Sie würden wollen
sie haben gewollt	sie hatten gewollt	sie würden wollen

SUBJUNCTIVE

PRESENT	PERFECT (1)
ich wolle	ich habe gewollt
du wollest	du habest gewollt
er/sie wolle	er/sie habe gewollt
wir wollen	wir haben gewollt
ihr wollet	ihr habet gewollt
Sie wollen	Sie haben gewollt
sie wollen	sie haben gewollt

IMPERFECT	PLUPERFECT (3)
ich wollte	ich hätte gewollt
du wolltest	du hättest gewollt
er/sie wollte	er/sie hätte gewollt
wir wollten	wir hätten gewollt
ihr wolltet	ihr hättet gewollt
Sie wollten	Sie hätten gewollt
sie wollten	sie hätten gewollt

INFINITIVE
PRESENT
wollen
PAST
gewollt haben

PARTICIPLE
PRESENT
wollend
PAST
gewollt

IMPERATIVE
woll(e)!
wollt!
wollen Sie!
wollen wir!

NOTE when preceded by an infinitive: *(1)* ich habe ... wollen *etc* *(2)* ich hatte ... wollen *etc* *(3)* ich hätte ... wollen *etc*

8. PREPOSITIONS

Prepositions are words such as 'from', 'in', 'with'. They are followed by nouns or pronouns, which, in German, must be in the case determined by the preposition. Many take only one case, but some are followed by one of two cases (see sections C and E).

The most common prepositions are given below in five categories according to whether they take the dative, the accusative, the genitive, the dative or accusative, or the genitive or dative case. They are listed in alphabetical order, with the generally accepted meanings on the left, a description of their use in brackets, and an illustration of usage.

A. WITH THE DATIVE ONLY

AUS

out of	(place)	**er lief aus dem Haus** he ran out of the house
from	(place)	**ich stamme aus Italien** I come from Italy
	(place)	**aus dieser Richtung** from this direction
	(time)	**ein Gemälde aus dem 18. Jahrhundert** a painting from the 18th century
	(cause)	**aus Langeweile** from boredom
made of	(material)	**aus Messing** made of brass

AUSSER

apart from		**außer einem Frosch habe ich keine Haustiere** apart from a frog I don't have any pets

190 PREPOSITIONS

out of		**außer Atem/Betrieb/Gefahr/ Kontrolle** out of breath/order/danger/control	
out	(idiom)	**wir essen nie außer Haus** we never eat out	

BEI

near	(place)	**er wohnt bei der Post** he lives near the post office
at	(place)	**bei mir/Ihnen/Schmidts** at my/your/the Schmidts' house
	(place)	**beim Bäcker** at the baker's
	(place)	**bei Woolworth** at Woolworth's
	(time)	**bei Tagesanbruch** at daybreak

Note: **bei** cannot be used with verbs of motion:

er übernachtet bei seiner Mutter
he's spending the night at his mother's

but: **er fährt gerade zu seiner Mutter**
he's on his way to his mother's

on	(time)	**bei seiner Ankunft/Abfahrt** on his arrival/departure
	(position)	**hat jemand Geld bei sich?** has anyone got any money on them?
with	(+pronoun)	**bei ihr war es anders** with her it was different
in	(with writers etc)	**bei Goethe/Shakespeare** in Goethe/Shakespeare
by	(time)	**bei Tag/Nacht** by day/night
	(+ gerund)	**er ist gerade beim Abwaschen** he's (just) washing up

PREPOSITIONS

GEGENÜBER

opposite/facing	(place)	**gegenüber dem Park/dem Park gegenüber** opposite the park
towards		**er ist mir gegenüber sehr freundlich** he's very friendly towards me
compared with		**ihm gegenüber ist sie fast ein Genie** compared with him she's practically a genius

---

GEMÄSS

in accordance with	**unseren Wünschen gemäß** in accordance with our wishes

---

MIT

with	(association)	**mit nur einem Löffel Zucker** with just one spoon of sugar
	(means)	**er geht mit einem Stock** he walks with a stick
		mit ihr ist heute nichts anzufangen you won't get anywhere with her today
by	(means)	**mit dem Auto/Flugzeug/Zug** by car/plane/train
at	(time)	**mit 30 Jahren** at 30 (years of age)
	(speed)	**mit 100 Stundenkilometern** at 100 kilometres an hour
in	(time)	**mit der Zeit** in (the course of) time

NACH

to	(place)	**der Zug nach Athen** the train to Athens
	(place)	**wer geht nach Hause?** who's going home?
	(place)	**nach rechts/links/oben/unten gehen** to go to the right/left/upstairs/downstairs
after	(time)	**nach der Prüfung/zwei Jahren** after the exam/two years
past	(time)	**es ist 5 (Minuten) nach 3** it's 5 (minutes) past 3
		meiner/Ihrer Meinung nach in my/your opinion

VON

from	(place)	**von Lübeck bis Hamburg** from Lübeck to Hamburg
	(place)	**von dieser Stelle aus kann man die Berge sehen** from this position you can see the mountains
	(place)	**wir holen dich vom (= von dem) Bahnhof ab** we'll collect you from the station
from	(time)	**von 6 bis 9 Uhr abends** from 6 to 9 in the evening
	(time)	**vom 1. bis zum 15. Juli** from 1st to 15th of July
of	(possession)	**ein Freund von mir** a friend of mine
		jeder/viele von uns each/many of us

Note: in colloquial language **von** is often used instead of the genitive case:

    die Erwartungen von deutschen Teenagern (= deutscher Teenager)
    the expectations of German teenagers

by	(agent)	**dieses Dorf wurde vom Feind zerstört** this village was destroyed by the enemy
	(agent)	**eine Platte von den Beatles** a record by the Beatles

ZU

to	(place)	**bitte, komm zu mir!** come to me, please!
	(place)	**wie komme ich zur (= zu der) Post?** how do I get to the post office?
	(place)	**er muß zum (= zu dem) Arzt** he has to go to the doctor's
at	(place)	**zu Hause sein** to be at home
	(time)	**zu Ostern/Weihnachten** at Easter/Christmas
	(time)	**zur Zeit** at present
	(price)	**zu 30 Pfennig das Stück** at 30 pfennigs each
	(price)	**zum halben Preis** at half price
for	(time)	**zum ersten Mal/zum erstenmal** for the first time
on	(manner)	**zu Fuß** on foot
	(+ gerund)	**sie kam kaum zum Schreiben** she hardly got round to writing

B. WITH THE ACCUSATIVE ONLY

BIS

till	(time)	**bis nächstes Jahr!** till next year!

Note: 'not till' is translated by **erst**:

ich fahre erst morgen in Urlaub
I'm not going on holiday till tomorrow

	(idiom)	**bis bald/später!** see you soon/later!
by	(time)	**bis morgen** by tomorrow

Note: **bis** is often coupled with other prepositions, which then determine the case of the following noun or pronoun:

bis zum 10. Juni   **bis an die Grenze**
by the 10th of June   as far as the border

but: **bis München**
as far as Munich

bis auf dich sind wir alle fertig
we're all ready except for you

DURCH

through	(place)	**er rannte durch das Dorf** he ran through the village
	(agent)	**ich habe sie durch meinen Vater kennengelernt** I got to know her through my father
	(means)	**nur durch Fleiß macht man Fortschritte** only through hard work do you make progress
by		**durch Zufall** by chance

ENTLANG
(usually with accusative)

along	(place)	**sie rannte die Straße entlang** she ran along the street

FÜR

for	(person)	**ich habe ein Geschenk für dich!** I have a present for you!
	(time)	**sie ging für ein Jahr ins Ausland** she went abroad for a year
	(price)	**wir haben es für 500 Mark bekommen** we bought it for 500 marks

GEGEN

against	(place)	**er lehnte sich gegen die Mauer** he leant against the wall
		was hast du gegen mich/diese Idee? what have you got against me/this idea?
about	(time)	**gegen 6 Uhr** at about 6 o'clock
towards	(time)	**gegen Abend/Ende des Monats** towards evening/the end of the month
in return for		**gegen Quittung bekommen Sie Ihr Geld zurück** you'll get your money back in return for your receipt
contrary to		**gegen alle Erwartungen** contrary to all expectations
for		**haben Sie Tabletten gegen Halsweh?** do you have any tablets for a sore throat?

196 PREPOSITIONS

OHNE

without

sie kam ohne ihre Eltern
she came without her parents

ohne mich!
count me out!

PER
(usually without a following article)

by

per Post
by post

ich bin per du mit ihr
I'm on first name terms with her

PRO
(usually without a following article)

zweimal pro Tag
twice a day

50 Pfennig pro Stück
50 pfennigs each

UM

round (place) **er fährt gerade um die Ecke**
he's just driving round the corner

(place) **wir alle standen um sie (herum)**
we all stood round her

at (time) **um 11 Uhr**
at 11 o'clock

around (time) **diese Kirche wurde um 1400 gebaut**
this church was built around 1400

um die Hälfte billiger
half as cheap

C. WITH THE DATIVE OR ACCUSATIVE

1. A number of German prepositions are followed by either the dative or accusative case. The most common are:

an	on(to), against, to, at, in
auf	(down) on(to)
hinter	behind
in	in(to)
neben	next to, beside
über	above, over
unter	under(neath), below
vor	in front of, before
zwischen	between

   As a general rule, the dative is used where the position or location of a person, thing or action is signified. **wo?** is thus the question word most likely to prompt a statement of this kind.

wo ist Katrin?	>	**sie sitzt auf dem Sofa**
where's Katrin?		she's sitting on the sofa
wo hängt der Spiegel?	>	**er hängt an der Tür**
where's the mirror (hanging)?		it's (hanging) on the door
wo kann man hier einen Spaziergang machen?	>	**im Park kann man einen Spaziergang machen**
where can you go for walk here?		you can go for a walk in the park

   The accusative indicates movement to, or in the direction of, a new position. **wohin?** is therefore the question word most likely to elicit a statement of this kind.

wohin fließt der Fluß?	>	**er fließt in den Bodensee**
where does the river flow to?		it flows into Lake Constance
wohin ist die Katze gesprungen?	>	**sie ist auf den Kühlschrank gesprungen**
where did the cat jump to?		it jumped onto the fridge

   The following short forms are very common, both in spoken and written German:

ans (= an das)	**am** (= an dem)
ins (= in das)	**im** (= in dem)

198 PREPOSITIONS

Other examples of abbreviation:

aufs (= auf das)	(**auf'm** (= auf dem) *used only in colloquial speech*)
hinters (= hinter das)	**hinterm** (= hinter dem)
übers (= über das)	**überm** (= über dem)
unters (= unter das)	**unterm** (= unter dem)
vors (= vor das)	**vorm** (= vor dem)

Note: there are no standard short forms with **neben** and **zwischen**, although in colloquial German, **nebens** (= neben das) is possible.

For the combination of prepositions with pronouns (**darin, darauf** etc) see p 89-90.

2. The following examples begin in each case with a pair of sentences to make clear the essential difference between these prepositions in their accusative and dative use:

ACCUSATIVE — **DATIVE**

AN

sie klebte das Foto an die Tür
he stuck the photo on the door

das Foto klebt an der Tür
the photo is stuck on the door

wir fliegen jeden Sommer ans Mittelmeer
we fly every summer to the Mediterranean

normalerweise zelten wir am Mittelmeer
we normally camp on the Mediterranean

on (time)
am Sonntag
on Sunday

(time)
am 31. August
on the 31st of August

in (time)
am Morgen/Abend
in the morning/ evening

(idiom)
an Ihrer Stelle
in your position

at (time)
am Wochenende
at the weekend

(place)
an einer Schule/Universität
at a school/ university

AUF

stellen Sie bitte Ihr Gepäck nicht auf das Bett!
please don't put your luggage on the bed

sie ist gerade auf ihr Zimmer gegangen
she's just gone to her room

mein Koffer steht aber nicht auf dem Bett
but my suitcase isn't on the bed

auf ihrem Zimmer schläft sie sicher bald ein
she'll soon fall asleep in her room

to (place)
auf den Markt gehen
to go to the market

(place)
er zieht aufs Land
he's moving to the country(side)

at (place)
auf dem Markt sein
to be at the market

in (place)
er wohnt auf dem Lande
he lives in the country(side)

(place)
auf einem Bild/der Welt
in a picture/the world

in (manner)
auf diese Weise
in this way

(language)
auf deutsch
in German

for (time)
auf einige Tage
for a few days

from (place)
auf 3 Kilometer zu sehen/hören
visible/audible from 3 kilometres

auf jeden Fall
whatever happens

auf einen Baum klettern
to climb a tree

HINTER

geh nicht hinter den Schrank!
don't go behind the wardrobe!

bitte setzen Sie sich hinter mich!
please sit behind me

ein Skelett steht hinter dem Schrank
there's a skeleton behind the wardrobe

nun sitzen alle hinter mir
now everyone's sitting behind me

after (place)
die erste Station hinter Stuttgart
the first stop after Stuttgart

die Behörden sind hinter ihnen her
the authorities are after them

beyond (place)
einige Kilometer hinter der Grenze
a few kilometres beyond the border

IN

unsere Katze kommt gern in die Küche
our cat likes coming into the kitchen

er geht in die Kirche/ins Kino/in den Zoo
he's going to church/to the the cinema/the zoo

to (place)
in die Alpen/die USA/ins Ausland reisen
to travel to the Alps/the USA/abroad

unsere Katze schläft gern in der Küche
our cat likes sleeping in the kitchen

er ist in der Kirche/im Kino/im Zoo
he's in church/at the cinema/the zoo

in (place)
in den Alpen/den USA/im Ausland arbeiten
to work in the Alps/the USA/abroad

PREPOSITIONS

Note:

    i) with most countries the relevant prepositions are **nach** and **in**:

        nach Schweden reisen   **in Schweden arbeiten**
        to travel to Sweden   to work in Schweden

    ii) compare 'I've never been to France/Switzerland'
       and 'ich war noch nie in Frankreich/in der Schweiz'

        in Urlaub fahren/gehen   **im Urlaub sein**
        to go on holiday   to be on holiday

in   (place)
gehen Sie in diese Richtung!   **gehen Sie in dieser Richtung weiter!**
go in this direction   keep going in this direction

Note: **wir fahren jetzt Richtung Moskau**
       we're travelling now in the direction of Moscow

schreib ihre Adresse in dein Notizbuch
write her address (down) in your notebook

in   (clothes)
in einen blauen Anzug gekleidet   **in Stiefeln/Blau gehen**
dressed in a blue suit   to wear boots/blue

into   (time)
es dauert bis spät in die Nacht (hinein)
it goes on (well) into the night

                                    in   (time)
                                           in einer Minute
                                           in one minute

                                           in der Nacht
                                           in the night

                                           im November/ Herbst
                                           in November/autumn

                                           im Jahre 1967
                                           in 1967

in (+ gerund)
im Vorbeigehen lächelte sie mich an
she smiled at me in passing

at
gut in Physik
good at physics

on
im Durchschnitt
on average

im Gegenteil
on the contrary

im ganzen
on the whole

NEBEN

sie setzte sich neben mich
she sat down beside me

sie saß neben mir
she was sitting beside me
er ging neben mir her
he walked beside me

compared with
neben meinen Schuhen sind deine sehr billig
compared with my shoes yours are very cheap

in addition to
neben diesen Kosten muß ich noch Mehrwertsteuer zahlen
in addition to these costs I also have to pay VAT

ÜBER

fahren Sie links über den Kanal
go left over the canal

ein Panzerwagen fährt über das Feld
a tank is driving across the field

via (place)
wir fliegen über die UdSSR nach China
we're flying to China via the USSR

through (agent)
das habe ich über einen Freund bekommen
I got it through a friend

over (time)
über eine Stunde
over (= *more than*) an hour

übers Wochenende
over the weekend

das ganze Jahr über
all year round

on/about
ein Buch über die deutsche Grammatik
a book on German grammar

for
ein Scheck über 100 Mark
a cheque for 100 marks

über dem Kanal lag dichter Nebel
there was thick fog over the canal

ein Hubschrauber kreiste über dem Haus
a helicopter was circling over the house

over (seniority)
sie steht über uns allen
she is over us all

but: **seit über einem Jahr wohne ich hier**
I've lived here for over a year

above
über dem Durchschnitt
above average

UNTER

das Flugzeug flog unter die Brücke
the plane flew under(neath) the bridge

er legte sich unter den Baum
he lay down underneath the tree

ich warte schon eine Stunde unter dieser Brücke
I've been waiting for an hour under this bridge

die Kinder spielten unter dem Baum
the children were playing under the tree

under (seniority)
Sie haben 2 Arbeiter unter sich
you have 2 workers under you

under (time)
unter 20 Jahren
under 20 (years of age)

in (idiom)
unter Umständen
in certain circumstances

under/less than
unter einem Kilo/einer Mark
under/less than a kilo/one mark

below
unter dem Meeresspiegel
below sea level

unter dem Durchschnitt
below average

among
unter ihren Freunden
among her friends

unter anderem
among other things

PREPOSITIONS 205

on (idiom)
unter der Bedingung, daß ...
on condition that ...

by
was versteht man unter 'Sex'?
what do you understand by 'sex'?

VOR

er setzt sich sofort vor den Fernseher
he immediately sits (himself) in front of the television

er sitzt den ganzen Abend vor dem Fernseher
he sits all evening in front of the television

vor ihm lag nichts als Schlamm
ahead of him lay nothing but mud

before (sequence)
A kommt vor B

before (time)
vor dem Krieg
before the war

vor dem 19. November
before 19th November

ago (time)
vor einem Jahr/einiger Zeit
a year/some time ago

to (time)
20 (Minuten) vor 6
20 (minutes) to 6

of (cause)
vor Hunger/Langeweile sterben
to die of hunger/boredom

PREPOSITIONS

with (cause)
vor Kälte zittern
to shiver with cold

grün vor Neid
green with envy

above (idiom)
vor allem/allen Dingen
above all

to (idiom)
er murmelte vor sich hin
he was mumbling to himself

ZWISCHEN

der Turm fiel zwischen zwei große Lastwagen
the tower fell between two big lorries

der Turm zwischen den jungen Bäumen steht noch
the tower between the young trees is still standing

between (time)
zwischen 4 und 5 Uhr
between 4 and 5 o'clock

Kinder zwischen 5 und 10 Jahren
children between 5 and 10 (years of age)

Note: **er ist zwischen 50 und 60 Jahre alt**
he's between 50 and 60 (years old)

(quantity)
zwischen 4 und 5 Mark pro Stunde
between 4 and 5 marks an hour

was ist der Unterschied zwischen Butter und Margarine
what's the difference between butter and margarine?

D. WITH THE GENITIVE

ANHAND

by means of	**er erläuterte seine Theorie anhand eines Beispiels** he explained his theory by means of an example

AUSSERHALB

outside	(place)	**eine Kirche steht außerhalb des Dorf(e)s** there's a church outside the village
	(time)	**außerhalb der Arbeitszeit** outside working hours

DIESSEITS

on this side of	(place)	**diesseits der Straße** on this side of the street

INNERHALB

inside	(place)	**innerhalb der Raumkapsel** inside the space module
within	(time)	**innerhalb einer Sekunde** within a second

JENSEITS

on the other side of	(place)	**jenseits des Flusses** on the other side of the river

KRAFT

by virtue of	**kraft seines Amtes** by virtue of his office

MITTELS

by means of	**mittels eines Zweitschlüssels** by means of a duplicate key

STATT

instead of		**statt des Bürgermeisters** instead of the mayor
	(idiom)	**statt dessen** instead of this/that

UM...WILLEN

...sake	**um ihrer Mutter willen** for her mother's sake
	um Gottes/Himmels willen! for God's/Heaven's sake!

WÄHREND

during	**während unseres Aufenthaltes in Italien** during our stay in Italy
	während dieser Zeit during this period

E. WITH THE GENITIVE OR DATIVE

DANK

thanks to	**dank meines guten Gedächtnisses**
	or **dank meinem guten Gedächtnis**
	thanks to my good memory

TROTZ

in spite of   **trotz strömenden Regens**
                  or **trotz strömendem Regen**
                  in spite of the pouring rain

Note: the use of the dative with **trotz** is generally regarded as colloquial. Note, however the following:

trotzdem   **trotz allem/alledem**
nonetheless   in spite of everything

which are standard German.

WEGEN
(usually before a noun)

because of   **wegen der hohen Preise**
                or **wegen den hohen Preisen**
                because of the high prices

...sake   **wegen meines Kindes**
                or **wegen meinem Kind**
                for my child's sake

Note: the use of the dative with **wegen** is generally regarded as colloquial.

Note the following forms with personal pronouns:

meinetwegen   **seinetwegen**   *etc*
for my sake   for his sake

Used colloquially, **meinetwegen** means 'as far as I'm concerned':

meinetwegen kann er auch mitkommen
as far as I'm concerned, he can come along too

9. CONJUNCTIONS

Conjunctions link words, phrases or clauses:

vor *und* hinter dem Haus
in front of *and* behind the house

schön *aber* gefährlich
beautiful *but* dangerous

nimm meinen Schirm, *damit* du nicht naß wirst
take my umbrella *so that* you don't get wet

They fall into two categories, co-ordinating and subordinating.

A. CO-ORDINATING CONJUNCTIONS

1. Definition

These link two similar words or groups of words (eg nouns, pronouns, adjectives, adverbs, prepositions, phrases or clauses).

2. The principal co-ordinating conjunctions:

aber	**denn**	**oder**
but	because	or
und	**sondern**	**sowie**
and	but	as well as

3. Word order

When introducing clauses they are followed by the normal word order:

ich esse gern Käse, aber ich trinke nicht gern Milch
I like cheese but I don't like milk

gehen wir ins Konzert, oder bleiben wir zu Hause?
shall we go to the concert, or shall we stay at home?

sie schlief nicht ein, sondern (sie) lag hellwach im Bett
she didn't go to sleep, but lay wide awake in bed

CONJUNCTIONS

Note: **sondern** is only used of two incompatible ideas.

nicht schwarz, sondern weiß
not black but white

nicht klug, sondern dumm
not clever but stupid

4. Conjunctions consisting of two parts:

sowohl ... als auch
both ... and

nicht nur ... sondern auch
not only ... but also

entweder ... oder
either ... or

weder ... noch
neither ... nor

sowohl deine Mutter als auch ich sind dagegen
both your mother and I are against it

nicht nur das Essen, sondern auch das Bier war sehr teuer
not only the food but the beer too was very expensive

entweder er oder sie muß weg
either he or she will have to go

weder Rom noch Neapel hat ihnen gefallen
they liked neither Rome nor Naples

5. Adverbs

Some adverbs also function as co-ordinating conjunctions. In such cases the order of the following subject and finite verb are reversed. Among the most common of these adverbs are:

also
so, therefore

außerdem
in any case

deshalb
therefore

inzwischen
meanwhile

sonst
otherwise

trotzdem
despite that

ich stehe morgen früh auf, ich muß also jetzt gehen
ich stehe morgen früh auf, also muß ich jetzt gehen
I'm getting up early tomorrow, so I'll have to go now

er steht heute unter Streß; er wäre sonst gekommen
er steht heute unter Streß; sonst wäre er gekommen
he's under pressure today, otherwise he would have come

sie ist 35; sie benimmt sich trotzdem wie ein Kind
sie ist 35; trotzdem benimmt sie sich wie ein Kind
she's 35; she behaves like a child despite that

B. SUBORDINATING CONJUNCTIONS

1. Definition

These join a subordinate clause to another clause, in particular a main clause. The finite verb comes at the end of a subordinate clause. (The only exception is noted in section 3b.)

2. The principal subordinating conjunctions:

daß that	**als** when	**bevor/ehe** before
nachdem after	**seit(dem)** since	**während** while
wenn if, when(ever)	**als ob** as if	**damit** so that
da/weil because	**so daß** with the result that	**sobald** as soon as
obwohl/obgleich although	**ohne (...) zu** without	**um (...) zu** in order to

bitte sag ihm, daß ich große Lust dazu hätte
please tell him that I'd love to do it

die Firma ging pleite, als sie 50 war
the firm went bust when she was 50

or **als sie 50 war, ging die Firma pleite**
when she was 50 the firm went bust

wenn wir nur Zeit hätten, würden wir so viel tun
if only we had the time we'd do so much

wenn ich dir begegne, siehst du immer so traurig aus
when(ever) I see you, you always look so sad

sie ging, als ob sie blind wäre
she was walking as if she were blind

CONJUNCTIONS 213

Note: **sie ging, als wäre sie blind** is also possible

mein Schirm war kaputt, so daß ich auf bis die Haut naß wurde
my umbrella was broken, so I got soaked

Note the difference between **so daß** and **damit**:

steh auf, damit ich dich sehe
stand up so (that) I can see you

Note: **ohne (...) zu** and **um (...) zu** + infinitive can only be used when the (implicit) subject is the same in each clause:

ohne ein Wort zu sagen, schlich er aus dem Haus
without saying a word, he crept out of the house

ich koche selber, um Geld zu sparen
I cook for myself to save money

3. Omission

On occasion, particularly in colloquial speech, a subordinating conjunction may be omitted.

a) When the subordinate clause in question comes after the main clause, the finite verb in it occupies its 'normal' position:

bitte sag ihm, ich hätte große Lust dazu
please tell him I'd love to do it

b) When the subordinate clause comes before the main clause, the finite verb in it is the first word of the sentence:

hätten wir nur Zeit, würden wir so viel tun
had we only the time, we'd do so much

Note that in all these examples the two clauses are still separated by a comma.

4. Interrogatives

Interrogatives (eg **was?**, **welcher?** and **wie?**) and **ob** function as subordinating conjunctions in indirect questions:

der Polizist fragte mich, ob ich etwas gehört hätte
the policeman asked me if I had heard anything

dann fragte er mich, was ich gehört hätte
then he asked me what I had heard

See also p 235-6.

10. NUMBERS AND QUANTITY

A. CARDINAL NUMBERS

0	null	30	dreißig
1	eins	40	vierzig
2	zwei	50	fünfzig
3	drei	60	sechzig
4	vier	70	siebzig
5	fünf	80	achtzig
6	sechs	90	neunzig
7	sieben	100	hundert
8	acht	101	hunderteins
9	neun	130	hundertdreißig
10	zehn	200	zweihundert
11	elf	257	zweihundertsiebenundfünfzig
12	zwölf		
13	dreizehn	1 000	tausend
14	vierzehn	1 001	tausend(und)eins
15	fünfzehn	1 234	tausendzweihundertvierunddreißig
16	sechzehn		
17	siebzehn *but:*	1990	neunzehnhundertneunzig (*date*)
18	achtzehn		
19	neunzehn	2 000	zweitausend
20	zwanzig	10 000	zehntausend
21	einundzwanzig	1 000 000	eine Million
26	sechsundzwanzig	1 198 269	eine Million hundertachtundneunzigtausendzweihundertneunundsechzig
		2 000 000	zwei Millionen
		1 000 000 000	eine Milliarde
		1 000 000 000 000	eine Billion

NUMBERS

Note:

a) The cardinal number 1 has the form **eins**

  i) in arithmetic:

  eins plus eins gleich zwei
  one plus one equals two

  ii) in compound numbers, when it is the last item:

  zweihunderteins   *but:*   **zweihunderteinundfünfzig**
  two hundred and one   two hundred and fifty one

  iii) after a noun:

  Zimmer eins   **Seite eins**
  room one   page one

b) When used before a noun it is declined like the indefinite article (see p 24), but distinguished from it by being printed in italics or stressed in speech:

  ich habe bloß *eine* Mark gespart!
  I only saved *one* mark!

but: if preceded by the definite article it is declined like a normal adjective, though in the singular only (see p 65)

  den einen Schein hat er schon, den anderen aber nicht
  he's got one certificate already, but not the other

Note:

  i) time expressions:

  um ein Uhr
  at one o'clock

  ii) expressions combined with **zwei**:

  jeden Tag liest er ein oder zwei Zeitungen
  every day he reads one or two papers

c) When used as a pronoun, 1 is declined like **dieser**:

  einer der Filme   **eines/eins der Bücher**
  one of the films   one of the books

d) **zwei** is sometimes replaced by **zwo** when it might be mistaken for **drei** (eg on the telephone).

NUMBERS

e) 'in twos', 'in threes' *etc* (up to 12) is translated by **zu zweit, zu dritt, zu viert, zu fünft** *etc*.

f) 'tens', 'twenties' *etc* as denominations of stamps and coins add the ending **-er** but are otherwise indeclinable, except for the dative plural:

   eine Zwanziger (Marke)   **ein Zwanziger (Schein)**
   a 20 pfennig stamp   a 20 mark note

g) 'dozens/hundreds/thousands of' is translated by

   Dutzende/Hunderte/Tausende von

h) Where English uses a comma in writing thousands *etc* German uses either a full stop or a space:

   1.500.000
   1 500 000
   1,500,000

The German for a million, a thousand million and a billion takes the plural form:

   zwei Millionen Mark/Wörter
   two million marks/words

B. ORDINAL NUMBERS

Note: the following numbers are usually preceded by an article etc and are always declined

1st	**erst-**
2nd	**zweit-**
3rd	**dritt-**
4th	**viert-**
5th	**fünft-**
6th	**sechst-**
7th	**siebt-**
8th	**acht-**
9th	**neunt-**
10th	**zehnt-**
11th	**elft-**
12th	**zwölft-**
13th	**dreizehnt-**
14th	**vierzehnt-**
15th	**fünfzehnt-**
16th	**sechzehnt-**
17th	**siebzehnt-**
18th	**achtzehnt-**
19th	**neunzehnt-**
20th	**zwanzigst-**
21st	**einundzwanzigst-**
30th	**dreißigst-**
100th	**hundertst-**
101st	**hunderterst-**
200th	**zweihundertst-**
1000th	**tausendst-**
10,000th	**zehntausendst-**
1,000,000th	**millionst-**

a) ordinal numbers agree with the noun following in gender and case:

meine zwölfte Stelle
my twelfth job

kennen Sie ihren sechsten Mann?
do you know her sixth husband?

NUMBERS

b) when written in figures, ordinals are followed by a full stop:

> **Beethovens 9. Symphonie**
> Beethoven's 9th symphony

> **heute ist der 23. Oktober**
> today is the 23rd of October

After the names of kings *etc* Roman numerals with punctuation, or, less commonly, the full form in words, are used:

> **das gehörte Karl V./Karl dem Fünften**
> that belonged to Charles V/Charles the Fifth

C. FRACTIONS AND PROPORTIONS

1. Fractions

Fractions are formed by substituting the **-te** ending of ordinal numerals by **-tel**. They are neuter nouns, but are only inflected in the genitive singular, adding **-s**:

ein Drittel	**vier Fünftel**	**zweidreiviertel**
a third (⅓)	four fifths (⅘)	two and three quarters (2¾)

but: half is translated either by **die Hälfte** (noun) or **halb-** (adjective or adverb):

die Hälfte der Studenten **die größere Hälfte**
half the students the larger half

eine halbe Stunde **ein halbes Kilo Äpfel**
half an hour half a kilo of apples

halb so viel **halb tot**
half as much half dead

Note: **anderthalb/eineinhalb**
one and a half

2. Decimals

The English decimal point is expressed as a comma in German:

zwei komma fünf (2,5)
two point five (2.5)

3. Arithmetic

addition:	**zwei plus/und drei gleich fünf**	2+3=5
subtraction:	**sieben minus/weniger eins gleich sechs**	7−1=6
multiplication:	**vier mal zwei gleich acht**	4×2=8
division:	**neun (geteilt) durch drei gleich drei**	9÷3=3
square:	**zwei hoch zwei gleich vier**	$2^2=4$

Note: **ist** or **sind** or **macht** are alternatives to **gleich**.

D. MEASUREMENTS AND PRICES

1. Measurements

a) *dimensions*

dieses Zimmer ist 4 Meter (4 m) lang und 3 Meter 70 (3,70 m) breit
this room is 4 metres long and 3.70 metres wide

das Loch ist 30 cm tief   **er ist 1,80 m groß**
the hole is 30 cm deep   he's 1.80 metres tall

b) *distance*

wie weit ist es von hier bis Kassel?
how far is it from here to Kassel?

bis Kassel sind es bloß 3 Kilometer
it's only 3 kilometres to Kassel

Kassel liegt 3 km von hier (entfernt)
Kassel is 3 km (away) from here

2. Prices

was kosten die Umschläge?
how much are the envelopes?

sie kosten zwei Mark zehn (DM 2,10)
they're 2 marks 10

diese Bananen haben mich 6 Mark gekostet!
these bananas cost me 6 marks!

75 Pfennig das/pro Stück
75 pfennigs each

5 Mark das/pro Kilo
5 marks a kilo

Weinbrand zu 15 Mark die/pro Flasche
brandy at 15 marks a bottle

das macht 34 Mark neunzig (DM 34,90)
that makes/comes to 34 marks 90

11. EXPRESSIONS OF TIME

A. THE TIME

    wie spät ist es?   **wieviel Uhr ist es?**
    what's the time?   what's the time?

    wieviel Uhr haben Sie?
    what do you make the time?

a) *full hours*

    es ist ein Uhr/eins   **es ist Mittag/Mitternacht**
    it's 1 o'clock   it's 12 noon (midday)/midnight

b) *half-hours* (note the difference from English)

    es ist halb vier   **es ist halb zwölf**
    it's half past three   it's 11.30

    es ist halb eins (nachts/nachmittags)
    it's 12.30 (at night/in the afternoon)

c) *quarter-hours*

    es ist Viertel nach elf/Viertel zwölf (*S. Germany*)
    it's 11.15

    es ist Viertel vor zehn/dreiviertel zehn (*S. Germany*)
    it's 9.45

d) *minutes*

    es ist acht Minuten nach neun
    it's 9.08

    es ist sechzehn Minuten vor sechs
    it's 5.44

    es ist fünf vor/nach halb drei
    it's 2.25/2.35

222 EXPRESSIONS OF TIME

    es ist zwanzig vor sieben
    it's 6.40

Note: **Uhr** is usually omitted, as is **Minuten** after 5, 10, 20 *etc*

e) *a.m. and p.m.*

    es ist zehn Uhr vormittags   **es ist drei Uhr nachmittags**
    it's 10 a.m.   it's 3 p.m.

Note: **es ist zwei Uhr nachts**   **es ist acht Uhr abends**
    it's 2 a.m.   it's 8 p.m.

f) the 24 hour clock is especially used in official announcements, TV and radio announcements, timetables *etc* but can also be used in ordinary speech:

    unser Zug fährt um 20 Uhr
    our train leaves at 8 p.m.

    die Vorstellung fängt um 19.30 Uhr an
    the performance starts at 7.30 p.m.

B. THE DATE

1. Names of months, days and seasons

a) *months (**die Monate**)*

Januar	January
Februar	February
März	March
April	April
Mai	May
Juni	June
Juli	July
August	August
September	September
Oktober	October
November	November
Dezember	December

b) *days of the week (**die Wochentage**)*

Montag	Monday
Dienstag	Tuesday
Mittwoch	Wednesday
Donnerstag	Thursday
Freitag	Friday
Samstag	Saturday
Sonnabend (*N. Germany*)	Saturday
Sonntag	Sunday

c) *seasons (**die Jahreszeiten**)*

der Frühling	spring
der Sommer	summer
der Herbst	autumn
der Winter	winter

Note: **im Juni**   **am Mittwoch**   **im Herbst**
in June   on Wednesday   in the autumn

2. Dates

a) Ordinal numbers are used for the dates of the month, as in English, but 'of' is not translated:

    der 1. (*spoken:* **erste**) **Mai**   **am 11.** (*spoken:* **elften**) **April**
    the first of May   on the 11th of April

Note: dates on letters and cards are usually written:

    Dortmund, (den) 3. 7. 1988 (*read* **den dritten siebten neunzehnhundertachtundachtzig**)
or   **Dortmund, den 3. Juli 1988**

b) 'what's the date today?' is translated as:

    der wievielte ist heute?
or   **den wievielten haben wir heute?**

c) With years, German either uses no preposition or the phrase **im Jahr(e)** + date:

    wir haben uns 1964/im Jahr(e) 1964 kennengelernt
    we got to know each other in 1964

d) Year dates are read as multiples of a hundred, except for years beginning with 10- and 20-:

	1100	**elfhundert**
	1984	**neunzehnhundertvierundachtzig**
but:	1066	**tausendsechsundsechzig**
	2001	**zweitausend(und)eins**

e) On wine labels years take an invariable **-er** ending:

    1976er Piesporter Michelsberg

EXPRESSIONS OF TIME

C. IDIOMATIC EXPRESSIONS

um 6 Uhr	at 6 o'clock
um 6 Uhr herum (*colloquial*)	round about 6 o'clock
gegen 10 Uhr	about/getting on for 10 o'clock
um Mitternacht	at midnight
um Mittag	at midday
Punkt 3 Uhr	on the stroke of three
es ist genau 3 Uhr	it's exactly 3 o'clock
es ist 5 Uhr vorbei	it's past 5 o'clock
ab 7 Uhr	from 7 o'clock on(wards)
von 9 bis 5 Uhr	from 9 to 5 o'clock
bleib bis 2 Uhr!	stay till 2 o'clock!
das muß bis 2 Uhr fertig sein	that must be ready by 2 o'clock!
kurz vor 8 Uhr	shortly before 8 o'clock
kurz nach 9 Uhr	shortly after 9 o'clock
eine Viertelstunde	a quarter of an hour
eine halbe Stunde	half an hour
eine Dreiviertelstunde	three quarters of an hour
morgens	in the morning, every morning
am Morgen	in the morning, every morning
am nächsten Morgen	(the) next morning
eines Morgens	one morning
(am) Montag morgen	on Monday morning
montags morgens	on Monday mornings
guten Morgen!	good morning!
abends	in the evening, every evening
am Abend	in the evening, every evening
(am) Samstag abend	on Saturday evening
samstags abends	on Saturday evenings
eines Abends	one evening
jeden Abend	every evening
guten Abend!	good evening!
nachts	at night
über Nacht	overnight
Nacht für Nacht	night after night
eines Nachts	one night
gute Nacht!	good night!

226 EXPRESSIONS OF TIME

heute	today
heute früh/morgen	this morning
heute nacht	last night/tonight
heutzutage	nowadays
gestern	yesterday
gestern abend	yesterday evening
vorgestern	the day before yesterday
gestern vor 8 Tagen	a week ago yesterday
morgen	tomorrow
morgen früh	tomorrow morning
übermorgen	the day after tomorrow
morgen in 8 Tagen	a week tomorrow
von heute auf morgen	at very short notice
am Sonntag	on Sunday
erst am Sonntag	not till Sunday
sonntags, jeden Sonntag	every Sunday
täglich (Tages-)	every day, daily
alltäglich (Alltags-)	everyday, mundane
in drei Tagen	in three days' time
tagsüber	during the day
letzte/nächste Woche	last/next week
vorletzte Woche	the week before last
übernächste Woche	the week after next
wöchentlich (Wochen-)	every week, weekly
während/unter der Woche	during the week
am/übers Wochenende	at/over the weekend
letzten/nächsten Monat	last/next month
monatlich (Monats-)	every month, monthly
zwei Monate lang	for two months
vor zwei Monaten	two months ago
er verdient 10 000 Mark im Monat	he earns 10,000 marks a month
Anfang/Ende März	at the beginning/end of March
letztes/nächstes Jahr	last/next year
jährlich (Jahres-)	every year, yearly
1900/im Jahr(e) 1900	in 1900
in den 60er Jahren	in the 60's
das Schaltjahr	leap year
im 19. Jahrhundert	in the 19th century
aus dem 15. Jh.	from the 15th century
mittelalterlich	medieval

EXPRESSIONS OF TIME

500 v.Chr. (= **vor Christus**)	500 BC
500 n.Chr. (= **nach Christus**)	500 AD
Ostern	Easter
Pfingsten	Whitsun
Weihnachten	Christmas
Silvester	New Year's Eve
er ist 18 Jahre alt	he's 18 (years old)
sie ist in den Zwanzigern	she's in her twenties
wir sind Mitte 40	we are in our mid 40s
in mittlerem Alter	middle-aged
in diesem Alter	at this/that age
das erste Mal	the first time
zum erstenmal	for the first time
meine Uhr geht vor/nach	my watch is fast/slow
der Zug hat 5 Minuten Verspätung	the train is 5 minutes late
im Augenblick	at the moment
früher oder später	sooner or later
mit der Zeit	in (the course of) time
im Laufe der Zeit	in (the course of) time
seit einiger Zeit	for some time past
eine Zeitlang	for a while
für/auf immer	for ever
Zeit verbringen	to spend time
Zeit vergeuden	to waste time
sich (*dat*) Zeit für etwas (*acc*) nehmen	to make time for something

12. THE SENTENCE

A. WORD ORDER

1. Main Clauses

a) In a simple sentence the basic word order is

    subject   finite verb (+ object/objects)   (+ complement)

wir essen   **wir essen unser Frühstück**
we're eating   we're eating our breakfast

wir essen unser Frühstück heute in der Küche
we're eating our breakfast today in the kitchen

b) If there is both a direct and an indirect object the normal order depends on whether they are nouns or pronouns

  i) two nouns (indirect, direct)

    er gab seiner Mutter das Buch
    he gave his mother the book/he gave the book to his mother

  ii) pronoun (indirect), noun (direct)

    er gab ihr das Buch
    he gave her the book

  iii) pronoun (direct), noun (indirect)

    er gab es seiner Mutter
    he gave it to his mother

  iv) two pronouns (direct, indirect)

    er gab es ihr
    he gave it to her

c) Past participles, dependent infinitives, separable prefixes and adverbial complements usually come at the end of a sentence:

> **sie hat ihn in Paris zum erstenmal gesehen**
> she saw him for the first time in Paris
>
> **Andrea will am Samstag eine Party veranstalten**
> Andrea wants to organize a party on Saturday
>
> **du lenkst mich von meiner Arbeit ab**
> you're distracting me from my work
>
> **das Spiel geriet heute völlig außer Kontrolle**
> the game got completely out of control today

Note: adverbial complements, in combination, come immediately before past participles, dependent infinitives and separable prefixes:

> **das Spiel ist heute völlig außer Kontrolle geraten**
> the game got completely out of control today

d) Inversion

It is far more common in German than in English to begin a sentence with something other than the subject. Not only adverbs and adverbial phrases but also direct and indirect objects regularly function in this way. Note, though, that only one such item may occur at the beginning of a given sentence.

i) If an adverb etc starts a sentence the finite verb must come immediately afterwards in second place (though it need not be the second word):

> **leider fällt der Unterricht heute aus**
> unfortunately there are no lessons today
>
> **die Hälfte des Personals hat man schon entlassen**
> they've already dismissed half the staff
>
> **auf den müssen Sie gut aufpassen!**
> you must keep a good eye on him!

ii) After inversion a pronoun subject must come directly after the finite verb:

> **endlich gab er mir meine Notizen zurück**
> he finally gave me back my notes

But a noun subject may either precede or follow a pronoun object:

morgen trifft meine Frau ihn am Flughafen
morgen trifft ihn meine Frau am Flughafen
my wife's meeting him at the airport tomorrow

iii) If a main clause comes second in a sentence inversion occurs:

wenn es schneit, machen wir einen Schneemann
if it snows we'll make a snowman

"alles Gute!" sagte sie zynisch
"all the best!", she said cynically

Note: after a **wenn** clause, **dann** may be added before the inverted main verb

2. Subordinate Clauses

After relative pronouns (**der**, **dessen**, **an dem**, **worauf** *etc*) and subordinating conjunctions (**daß**, **warum**, **obwohl** *etc*) the finite verb goes to the end of the clause:

das ist das Kind, dessen Eltern beide Teenager sind
that's the child whose parents are both teenagers

kennen Sie Otto, mit dem ich jahrelang in Urlaub gefahren bin?
do you know Otto, who I've been going on holiday with for years?

When two subordinate clauses follow the same conjunction, remember to put the verb at the end of *both*:

wenn er morgen kommt und die Leitung endlich repariert ...
if he comes tomorrow and finally repairs the pipes ...

Note: if two infinitive forms occur together with a finite (auxiliary) verb, this latter verb comes first:

er weiß, daß er es nicht hätte tun sollen
he knows that he should not have done it

Note: if a subordinate clause is interrupted by another clause the word order is not affected:

sie heiratet einen Mann, der, obwohl er nicht reich ist, wenigstens gut aussieht
she's marrying a man who, although he's not rich, is at least good-looking

B. NEGATIVES

1. Main negative words

kein, keine, kein (*indef art*)	not a, no
keiner, keine, kein(e)s (*pron*)	nobody, none
keinerlei	no ... of any sort
keineswegs	by no means
nicht	not
nicht nur ... sondern auch	not only ... but also
nicht mehr	no more
nichts	nothing
nie, niemals	never
niemand	nobody
nirgends, nirgendwo	nowhere
nirgendwohin	(to) nowhere
weder ... noch	neither ... nor

2. Position of *nicht*

a) **nicht** follows the finite verb it refers to:

    ich fluche nicht   **du darfst nicht rauchen**
    I don't swear   you're not allowed to smoke

b) If there is an object, **nicht** follows it:

    er braucht seine Eltern nicht   **du hörst mir nicht zu**
    he doesn't need his parents   you're not listening to me

    sie hat ihrer Mutter den Brief nicht gegeben
    she didn't give her mother the letter

c) **nicht** precedes a noun phrase or pronoun if a contrast is involved:

    gib dies nicht deinem Bruder, sondern deiner Schwester
    don't give this to your brother but to your sister

    ich will nicht die blauen Blumen, sondern die gelben
    I don't want the blue flowers, I want the yellow ones

    ich will die gelben Blumen, nicht die blauen
    I want the yellow flowers, not the blue ones

Note: If there is inversion, **nicht** can occur in more than one position:

    nicht die blauen Blumen will ich, sondern die gelben
    die blauen Blumen will ich nicht, sondern die gelben

3. 'not a', 'not any', 'no' + noun are usually translated by **kein-**, ie. **nicht** is not normally used together with **ein**:

> **sie braucht keinen Mann**
> she doesn't need a husband
>
> **ich habe keine Reiseschecks**
> I haven't got any traveller's cheques
>
> **keine Politesse war zu sehen**
> there was no traffic warden in sight

The emphatic 'not a (single)' is translated by **kein- einzig-**:

> **kein einziger Baum blieb stehen**
> not a (single) tree was left standing

Note: **nicht** may occur with **ein** when **ein** means one and a contrast is involved:

> **sie haben uns nicht eine, sondern zwei Flaschen gebracht**
> they have brought us not one, but two bottles

THE SENTENCE

C. DIRECT AND INDIRECT QUESTIONS

1. Direct questions

There are four basic ways of forming direct questions in German:

a) *inversion of the normal word order of a statement:*

rauchen Sie? **schläft sie?** **regnet es?**
do you smoke? is she asleep? is it raining?

liebst du mich? **sprechen Sie Deutsch?**
do you love me? do you speak German?

schneit es noch?
is it still snowing?

darf ich Ihnen meinen Mann vorstellen?
may I introduce my husband to you?

ist es letztes Jahr ins Englische übersetzt worden?
was it translated into English last year?

b) *question word(s) + finite verb (+ subject) (+ complement)*

wer?	**(an) wen?**	**wessen?**	**(mit** *etc***) wem?**
who?	(to) who(m)?	whose?	(with *etc*) whom?

wann? **warum?** **was?**
when? why? what?

was für? **welch-?** **wie?**
what kind of? which? how?

wo? **woher?** **wohin?**
where? where ... from? where ... to?

Note: for **wo** + preposition (eg. **womit?**) see p 107.

wer kommt? **wessen Hut ist das?**
who's coming? whose hat is that?

mit wem spielt sie?
who is she playing with?

wann geht er? **warum kannst du nicht schlafen?**
when is he going? why can't you sleep?

was siehst du dort? **wohin fahren wir?**
what do you see there? where are we going?

welche Bluse steht mir besser?
which blouse suits me better?

wie heißt das auf deutsch?
what's that in German?

Note: the case after **was für** is determined by the preceding preposition or by the following noun's grammatical function, not by the word **für**:

bei was für einer Firma arbeitet sie?
in what kind of firm does she work?

was für ein Mann könnte so etwas tun?
what kind of man could do such a thing?

c) *subject + finite verb (+ complement)*

With colloquial questions of this kind, expressing disbelief, the pitch of the voice is raised on the key word, which is also emphasized.

Oma **tanzt?!**   **Oma** *tanzt?!*
Granny's dancing?!   Granny's *dancing?!*

das soll *billig* **sein?!**
that's supposed to be *cheap*?!

Horst wurde heute nachmittag zum *Vorsitzenden* **ernannt?!**
Horst was appointed *chairman* this afternoon?!

d) *subject + finite verb (+ complement) + tag*

In English there are many question tags, e.g. 'isn't it?', 'aren't you?', 'doesn't he?', 'can't she?', 'wouldn't we?', 'mightn't they?' *etc*. By comparison there are fewer question tags in German.

i) nicht (wahr)?

nicht (wahr)? is normally used at the end of a sentence when confirmation of a statement is expected. It is often shortened to just **nicht?**, especially in colloquial speech. Only the full form can stand at the beginning of a sentence, though this is uncommon:

es ist furchtbar kalt heute, nicht (wahr)?
it's terribly cold today, isn't it?

gestern haben wir viele Fehler gemacht, nicht (wahr)?
yesterday we made lots of mistakes, didn't we?

nicht wahr, sie gehört in die Mannschaft?
she should be in the team, shouldn't she?

ja? is an alternative for **nicht wahr?** at the end of a sentence:

du kommst heute abend, ja?
you're coming this evening, aren't you?

ii) **gell?/gelt?**

In Southern Germany and Austria **gell?** or **gelt?** is frequently found in colloquial speech as an alternative to the above:

Münchner Bier schmeckt gut, gell?
Munich beer tastes good, doesn't it?

iii) **oder?**

oder? at the end of a sentence invites confirmation or a response:

du ißt doch Fleisch, oder?
you do eat meat, don't you?
letzten Sonntag haben wir nicht gespielt, oder?
we didn't play last Sunday, (or) did we?

2. Indirect questions

a) *definition*

Indirect questions follow a verb or a clause and are introduced by an interrogative word, eg:

explain why you're angry   I asked her who she was

b) *word order*

German word order and punctuation differ from English. The two clauses are always separated by a comma and the finite verb comes at the end of the indirect question.

i) when the 'original' sentence contains an interrogative (eg. **wann? warum? was für?**):

wann geben Sie Ihr nächstes Konzert?	> **man fragt, wann Sie Ihr nächstes Konzert geben**
when are you going to give your next concert?	people are asking when you are going to give your next concert
warum gefällt es euch nicht?	> **sagt mal, warum es euch nicht gefällt**
why don't you like it?	tell me why you don't like it

was für Kinder unterrichten Sie? >	**er möchte wissen, was für Kinder Sie unterrichten**
what kind of children do you teach?	he wants to know what kind of children you teach

ii) when the 'original' sentence does not contain an interrogative the indirect question is introduced by **ob**:

kann er Deutsch? >	**ich bin gespannt, ob er Deutsch kann**
can he speak German?	I'm curious to know if he can speak German
hast du gut geschlafen? >	**sie hat mich gefragt, ob ich gut geschlafen hätte**
did you sleep well?	she asked me if I had slept well

Note: Occasionally it is necessary, as in English, to change the pronouns and the tense (and mood) of the verb in the indirect question from those of the 'original' direct question. For the correct sequence of tenses see p 145.

THE SENTENCE

D. ANSWERS ('YES' AND 'NO')

1. JA and NEIN

a) **ja** means 'yes' and is equivalent to longer positive answers such as: 'yes, it is', 'yes, I will', 'yes, he has' *etc*:

gehst du schon?	**ja(, ich muß jetzt gehen)**
are you going already?	yes(, I have to go now)

Note: **ja** can be emphasized in a number of ways:

  i) by being repeated (**ja, ja!**) with the stress on the second **ja**

  ii) in combination with **wohl**: **jawohl!** (= 'yes, indeed'), especially in the armed forces

b) **nein** means 'no' and is equivalent to longer negative answers such as: 'no, it isn't', 'no, I didn't' *etc*:

war es interessant?	**nein(, es war langweilig)**
was it interesting?	no(, it was boring)

Note: **nein** and **ja** used with **glauben/denken** translates '(don't) think so':

regnet es?	**ich glaube nein/ich glaube ja**
is it raining?	I don't think so/I think so

2. JA or DOCH?

ja and **doch** both mean 'yes', but **ja** is used to answer an affirmative question, and **doch** to contradict a negative question:

ist dieser Platz frei?	**ja**
is this seat taken?	yes(, it is)
liebst du mich nicht mehr?	**doch**
don't you love me any more?	yes(, I do love you)

13. TRANSLATION PROBLEMS

A. GENERAL TRANSLATION PROBLEMS

1. English words not translated in German and vice versa

a) Articles

  i) The indefinite article is often left out in German where it is present in English (see p 24-5):

   er ist leider Popsänger geworden
   unfortunately he's become a pop singer

  ii) The definite article is often used where it is omitted in English, especially with abstract nouns (see p 20):

   ich verstehe nichts von der Gärtnerei
   I know nothing about gardening

b) **daß** and the relative pronoun (see p 212 and 103-6)

  These are often omitted in English but must be kept in German:

   er bestand darauf, daß ich komme
   he insisted I come

   das Getränk, das ich am liebsten mag
   the drink I like best

  Except for the **daß** introducing indirect statements, which is optional (see p 213):

   er behauptete, daß er krank wäre
   er behauptete, er wäre krank
   he claimed he was ill

TRANSLATION PROBLEMS

c) After modal verbs a verb expressing motion is very often omitted if there is an adverb or phrase indicating direction (see p 156):

ich muß nach Hause	**willst du mit ins Kino?**
I have to go home	do you want to come to the cinema?

d) 'can' is sometimes omitted with verbs of perception where it is present in English:

hörst du mich?	**ich spüre nichts**
can you hear me?	I can't feel anything

e) German has many adverbs which intensify the meaning of the sentence as a whole. Very often there is no direct, word for word equivalent in English. Common examples are **ja**, **aber**, sometimes **doch**, **schon**, **wohl**:

du hast es ja gefunden!	**das ist aber gescheit!**
you've found it!	that *is* clever
das wäre wohl besser	**du verstehst schon?**
that *would* be better	you do understand?

2. Other differences

a) *es*

  i) **es** is used as an object with verbs where English has 'so' (see p 89):

du hast es gesagt!	**sie hat es getan**
you said so	she did so

  ii) **es** is used with **sein** to refer back to a previous word or clause where there is no equivalent in English:

  sie soll ehrlich sein und sie ist es auch
  she's said to be honest and she is

  iii) Note the different word order from English:

  ich bin es
  it's me

Note: 'it' must be translated by **er**, **sie** or **es** depending on the gender of the noun it refers to:

die Wurst stinkt; willst du sie wirklich essen?
this sausage smells; do you really want to eat it?

b) 'my', 'you' etc

The English possessive article (my *etc*) is often translated by the definite article with parts of the body and clothes (see p 21):

wasch dir die Hände! **der Hut flog ihm vom Kopf**
wash your hands his hat flew off his head

c) *commas*

i) In German do not put commas round an adverb within a clause:

plötzlich fuhr er hoch
suddenly, he jumped up

mein Vater wollte natürlich mitspielen
my father, of course, wanted to join in

ii) In German a comma is always put between two clauses except:

★ when there is a common subject, conjunction or verb which is not repeated:

er fiel und verstauchte sich den Fuß
he fell and twisted his ankle

weil er schneller laufen und also wahrscheinlich gewinnen kann
because he can run more quickly and can therefore probably win

★ it *may* be omitted before **und**, **aber**, **oder** when the same subject is repeated:

ich werde ihn sehen und ich werde es ihm sagen
I will see him and I will tell him

But this is only in shorter sentences; otherwise the comma is normally included, even before **und** or **oder** between clauses with the same subject:

wir müssen vorsichtig sein, oder wir verlieren alles
we'll have to be careful or we'll lose everything

du gehst sofort nach Hause, und du bleibst dort, bis ich anrufe
you're to go straight home and stay there until I ring up

iii) If the subject word changes, a comma must be inserted even if the subject word refers to the same person or thing:

der Stuhl ist alt, aber er ist bequem
the chair is old but it is comfortable

meine Frau kommt, und sie will dich sprechen
my wife is coming and she wants to speak to you

d) *agreement of subject and verb*

In English, words which are singular in form can have a plural meaning and can be used with either a singular or a plural verb: 'the government thinks/think, the team has/have' *etc.* In German the verb must be singular:

die Regierung beabsichtigt   **die Mannschaft hat gewonnen**
the government intend(s)   the team has (have) won

e) *direct speech*

There are various ways of punctuating direct speech in German:

"was machst du da?" fragte sie
"what are you doing there?" she asked

„was machst du da?" fragte sie
"what are you doing there?" she asked

« was machst du da? » fragte sie
"what are you doing there?" she asked

The last version is mostly used in print.

If 'she asked' comes at the beginning then a colon is used with all three options being available:

sie fragte: "was machst du da?"
she asked, "what are you doing there?"

B. SPECIFIC TRANSLATION PROBLEMS

1. English verbs ending in -ing

a) As part of a continuous tense it is translated by the appropriate German tense:

he's speaking	**er spricht**
he was speaking	**er hat gesprochen/er sprach**
he had been speaking	**er hatte gesprochen**
he will be speaking	**er spricht/er wird sprechen**
he would be speaking	**er würde sprechen**

The first three often have **gerade** added:

er spricht gerade *etc*

b) In German the -ing form is seldom used as a predicate adjective, after the verb, as in: 'he found the film disappointing'. This usage can often be translated by the verb in its finite form:

der Film enttäuschte ihn
he found the film disappointing

c) As an adverb, the German usage is often the same as English:

"ich habe gewonnen!" sagte er lachend
"I've won," he said, laughing

d) The English -ing form used as a subject or object can often be translated by the German infinitive made into a noun:

sein Erscheinen überraschte mich
his coming surprised me

e) An infinitive with **zu** may also be used:

das zu sagen bringt uns nicht voran
saying that won't help

du solltest versuchen, ihn zu überzeugen
you should try convincing him

f) Very often the -ing structure has to be translated into German by a subordinate clause:

> **er lockte die Kunden an, indem er den Preis einiger Artikel senkte**
> he attracted customers by lowering the price of a few items
>
> **dadurch, daß sie uns den Raum anbot, hat sie alles ermöglicht**
> by offering us the room she made everything possible

g) With verbs of perception (seeing, hearing, feeling *etc*), a **wie** clause is common:

> **ich beobachte, wie er sich versteckte**
> I saw him hiding
>
> **sie fühlte, wie das Kind sich an sie schmiegte**
> she felt the child snuggling up to her

h) Adverbial phrases of time with a verb in the -ing form very often become a subordinate clause in German:

> **bevor er hinausging, schloß er beide Türen ab**
> before going out, he locked both doors
>
> **als er die Fußgängerzone überquerte, traf er einen alten Freund**
> crossing the pedestrian precinct, he met an old friend

Similar phrases are also often translated by two main clauses joined by **und**:

> **er schloß beide Türen sorgfältig ab und ging hinaus**
> carefully closing both doors, he went out

i) A German relative clause may also be the equivalent of an English phrase with -ing:

> **die Polizei sucht eine blonde Frau, die eine grüne Tasche trägt**
> the police are looking for a fair-haired woman carrying a green bag

2. 'there is/are'

a) German usage often avoids direct translation, preferring one of a number of verbs:

> **die Zeitung liegt auf dem Sofa**
> there's a newspaper on the sofa

um die Ecke steht ein Parkhaus
there's a multi-storey garage round the corner

überall herrschte Freude
there was joy everywhere

ich hätte eine Frage an dich
there's something I want to ask you

b) *es gibt*

es gibt is typically used in statements about the fact that something exists (or doesn't exist) in a general sense. It is followed by nouns or pronouns, both singular or plural, in the accusative case. Note also **es gab, es hat(te) gegeben, es wird geben** *etc*:

es gibt keine Giftschlangen in Irland
there are no poisonous snakes in Ireland

zur Zeit gibt es einen Überschuß an Stahl in der EG
at present there's a surplus of steel in the EEC

es gab damals wenig zu tun
there was little to do in those days

so was gibt es nicht mehr!
there's no such thing any more!

Note the following idiomatic uses of **es gibt**:

was gibt's?	**heute abend gibt es Milchreis**
what's up?	there's rice pudding this evening

c) *es ist, es sind*

These are used to indicate presence, often temporary, in a defined space. **es ist** is followed by a singular and **es sind** by a plural, both in the nominative case. With inversion **es** disappears. Note also **es war(en)** *etc*:

es ist jemand an der Tür
there's someone at the door

es sind Würstchen im Kühlschrank
there are sausages in the fridge

Herr Ober, in meiner Suppe ist eine Fliege!
waiter, there's a fly in my soup!

in der Stadt war nicht viel los
there wasn't much happening in the town

Note: **es war einmal ...**
once upon a time ...

3. Expressions of place

German distinguishes very precisely whether an expression of place indicates position or motion — and if motion, then whether towards or away from the speaker by attaching either **her** or **hin**:

wo bist du? **wohin gehst du?**
where are you? where are you going?

woher kommst du?
where do you come from?

sag mir, wohin du gehst
tell me where you are going

komm herein!	**komm hierher!**	**bleib hier!**
come in	come here	stay here
es ist dort	**es kommt dorthin!**	**er ist oben**
it's there	it goes there	he's upstairs

sie bleibt draußen **die Kirche steht links**
she's staying outside the church is on the left

komm nach oben! **geh schnell nach draußen!**
come upstairs go outside quickly

dann gehen Sie nach links
then you go left

es ist innen schon gestrichen
it's already been painted inside

die Tür geht nach innen auf
the door opens inwards

sie warten schon drinnen
they're waiting inside

sie sitzt hinten **er ging nach hinten**
she's at the back he went to the back

4. 'to put'

German very often translates 'to put' by a more specific verb indicating precisely how the object is put, i.e. whether it is set down, laid down *etc*:

a) *legen* means the object lies:

sie legte ihre Hand auf seinen Kopf
she put her hand on his head

> **er legte die Zeitung auf den Stuhl**
> he put the newspaper on the chair

b) *setzen* means the object sits:

> **er setzte das Kind aufs Töpfchen**
> he put the child on the potty

Note also:

> **hier mußt du ein Komma setzen**
> you have to put a comma here

c) *stecken* means the object goes inside something:

> **er steckte den Schlüssel ins Schloß**
> he put the key in the lock
>
> **der Spion steckte die Papiere ins Geheimfach**
> the spy put the papers in the secret compartment
>
> **sie steckten ihn für drei Jahre ins Gefängnis**
> they put him into prison for three years

d) *stellen* means the object stands:

> **er stellte die Milch in den Kühlschrank**
> he put the milk into the fridge
>
> **wir haben den Mahagonitisch ins Wohnzimmer gestellt**
> we've put the mahogany table in the living room

e) *tun* is the most general term for 'to put'; it is slightly colloquial:

> **er tat das Geld schnell in die Tasche**
> he quickly put the money in his pocket
>
> **tun Sie das bitte wieder weg**
> put it away again, please

5. 'all the'

'all the' followed by a singular noun is usually translated by **ganz** rather than **all der** *etc*:

> **die ganze Mannschaft**   **das ganze Geld**
> all the team   all the money

6. The passive

The passive tends to be less common in German than in English. It is often replaced by **man**:

> **das tut man nicht**
> that isn't done
>
> **man behauptet, er habe das Geld gestohlen**
> he is said to have stolen the money

lassen can be used with an infinitive which has a passive sense (see p 141):

> **das läßt sich machen**
> that can be done
>
> **ich lasse das Zimmer neu tapezieren**
> I'm having the room freshly decorated

The active form with the agent (by . . .) as the subject is often used:

> **viele hielten Pele für den besten Fußballspieler der Welt**
> Pele was believed by many to be the best footballer in the world

7. 'when'

a) For a single event in the present or future: **wenn**

> **wenn ich bald nach New York fliege, nehme ich dich mit**
> when I fly to New York soon I'll take you with me
>
> **wenn wir in Zukunft nichts zu tun haben, ruhen wir uns aus**
> in future, when we have nothing to do we're going to relax

b) For a repeated action or state in present, past or future: **wenn**

> **wenn er abends Hunger hat, ißt er immer Erdnüsse**
> when(ever) he's hungry in the evening he always eats peanuts
>
> **wenn die Sonne schien, pflegten wir im Freien zu spielen**
> whenever the sun shone we used to play out of doors

c) For a single event in the past: **als**

> **als wir euch zum ersten Mal sahen, bekamen wir einen Schock**
> when we saw you for the first time we got a shock
>
> **als ich sechs Jahre alt war, konnte ich noch nicht lesen**
> when I was six I still couldn't read

d) For questions: **wann**

> **wann war das?**
> when was that?
>
> **wann gehst du endlich ins Bett?**
> when are you eventually going to go to bed?
>
> **ich möchte wissen, wann du endlich ins Bett gehst**
> I'd like to know when you're eventually going to go to bed

Note: In indirect statements **wann** is used following verbs of saying and many similar, even if a question is not implied:

> **er hat mir erzählt, wann er die Entdeckung machte**
> he told me when he made the discovery
>
> **ich habe vergessen, wann er sie getroffen hat**
> I have forgotten when he met her

INDEX

a, an 24
aber 210
abstract nouns 9, 20, 45
accusative 9, 53
active 9
addition 219
adjectival nouns 9, 44-6
adjectives 9, 62-76, 101-2, 151
adverbs 10, 77-85, 211
agreement 10, 62-4, 103-4
all 33-4
all the 84, 246
alle 33-4
als 212-3, 247
als ob 143, 212
als wenn 143
also 211
am 19, 197
a.m. 222
an 164, 198
and 210
anderthalb 219
anhand 207
ans 19, 197
anstatt 149
answers 237
anyone 92-3
apposition 10
articles 10, 18-38, 238
at 190
attributive 62
auf 164, 199
aufs 19, 198
aus 165, 189
außer 90, 189-90
außerdem 211
außerhalb 90, 207
auxiliary 10

be- 135

because 212
before 205, 212
bei 190
beide 98-9
beim 19
bevor 212
bis 90, 194
bißchen 97
brauchen 148
but 210

capital letters 39, 45
cardinal numbers 10, 214-6
cases 10, 53-4, 87
clause 11
collectives 11, 51
colloquial 11
colours 45-6, 51-2
commas 240-1
comparative 11, 72-4, 84
comparative adjectives 72-4
comparative adverbs 84
comparison 72
compound 11
compound nouns 11
conditional 11, 115-6
conditional sentences 142-3
conjugation 12, 111-30
conjunctions 12, 210-13
co-ordinating conjunctions 210-1
countries 43, 64

da 212
dagegen 89
damit 89, 212-3
dank 209
daran 89
daraus 89
das (article) 18-9
das (pronoun) 103

dasjenige 28, 66
daß 212, 238
dasselbe 28, 66
date 223-4
dative 12, 54
dative object 162-3
days of the week 223
decimals 219
declension 12, 55-61
definite article 12, 18-23, 103
dein 37-8
deiner 86
dem 18-9, 103
demonstratives 12, 30-6
demonstrative pronouns 30-6
den 18, 103-4
denen 103-4
denn 210
der (article) 18-23
der (pronoun) 103-4
deren 23, 103
derer 23
dergleichen 29
derjenige 28, 66
derselbe 28, 66
deshalb 211
dessen 23, 103
dich 87
die (article) 18-23
die (pronoun) 103-4
diejenige 28, 66
diese 30-1, 66
dieselbe 28, 66
dieser 66
dieses 66
diesseits 207
dimensions 220
dir 86
direct object 12
distance 220
division 219
doch 237
double prefixes 136
Drittel 219
du 86

durch 194
dürfen 124-5, 152

each 30
ehe 212
ein 24-5
eine 24-5
einem 24-5
einen 24-5
einer 24-5
eines 24-5
einige 101
einiges 101-2
eins 214-5
either ... or 211
emp- 135
ending 12
ent- 135
entlang 195
entweder ... oder 211
er 86
er- 135
es 86, 88-9, 239
es gibt 159, 244
es ist 159, 244
es sind 244
etwas 95-6
euer 37
even 84
every 30-1
exclamation 13
exclamation marks 114, 141
expressions of time 221-7
expressions of place 245

feminine 13, 41-2
finite 13
for 195
formation of compound tenses 131-3
fractions and proportions 219
from 192
für 195
future tense 113
future passive 116

INDEX

future perfect 113
future perfect passive 116

ge- 135
gegen 195
gegenüber 90
gemäß 191
gender 13, 39-47, 88
genitive 13, 54
geographical names 20

haben 111, 115, 131-2
halb 217, 221
half 217
half past 221
Hälfte 219
Herr 60
hinter 200
hinters 198
historic present 138
hours 221
how 233
hundert 214

ich 86
idiomatic 13
if 212
ihm 86
ihn 86
Ihnen 86
ihr (personal pronoun) 86
ihr (possessive) 37
Ihr 37
ihrer 86
Ihrer 86
im 19, 197
immer+**comparative** 84
imperative 13, 141-2
imperfect tense 112, 119, 124
imperfect subjunctive 115, 122-3, 127
imperfect passive 116
impersonal verbs 157-9
in 200-2
indefinite 13

indefinite article 13, 24-6, 67-8
indefinite pronoun 92-4
indicative 14
indirect object 14, 54
indirect questions 233-6
indirect speech 144-6
infinitive 14, 115, 146-50
infinitive with *zu* 149-50
-ing forms 242-3
innerhalb 90, 207
ins 19, 197
inseparable prefixes 135
interrogatives 14, 213
interrogative pronouns 107
intransitive verbs 132
inversion 229-30
inverted commas 241
inzwischen 211
irgendein 25-6
irgendwelche 26, 66
irregular verbs see **strong verbs**
isn't it? 234-5

ja 237
jede 30
jedermann 97-8
jemand 92-3
jene 30-1
jenseits 207

kein 27, 231-2
keiner 27, 231
keinerlei 231
keineswegs 231
können 124-8, 153
kraft 207

lassen 147-8, 161
legen 245-6
letter writing 86

main clauses 228-30
man 25, 92
manche 30, 66
manner 82

252 INDEX

many a 31-2
masculine 14, 39-40
measurements 220
mehrere 101
mein 37
meiner 37, 86
meinesgleichen 93
Mensch 21
mich 86
minutes 221-2
mir 86
miß- 135
mit 165, 191
mit- 135
mittels 208
mixed verbs 128-30
modal verbs 124-8
mögen 124-5, 153-4
months 21, 223
mood 14, 110
multiplication 219
müssen 124-5, 154

nach 165, 192
nachdem 212
neben 202
negatives 231-2
nein 237
neither ... nor 211, 231
neuter 14, 42-4
never 231
nicht 231
nicht nur ... sondern auch 211, 231
nichts 96-7, 231
nicht wahr? 234
nie 231
niemals 231
niemand 92, 231
nirgends 231
no 231, 237
nobody 92, 231
noch 84
nominative 14, 53
none 231

no-one 92
not 231
not a 231
nothing 231
nouns 14, 39-61
nowhere 231
null 214
number 15
numbers 214-20

ob 213
object 15
obwohl 212
oder 210
of 54, 192
ohne 90, 196, 212
on 199
or 210
ordinal numbers 217-8

paar 95
participles 63, 77, 151-2
passive 15, 116, 141-2, 247
passive infinitive 117
past participle 15, 117, 123
per 196
perfect tense 112, 120, 125
perfect infinitive 117
perfect infinitive passive 117
perfect passive 116
perfect subjunctive 115, 123, 127
person 15
personal pronouns 86-90
place 82
pluperfect tense 113, 120, 125
pluperfect passive 116
pluperfect subjunctive 115, 123, 128
plurals 15, 48-52
p.m. 222
possessive 15
possessive pronouns 37-8
predicative 62
prefixes 135-6
prepositions 16, 104, 189-209

INDEX 253

prepositions with the accusative 194-6
prepositions with the dative 189-93
prepositions with the dative or accusative 197-206
prepositions with the genitive 207-8
prepositions with the genitive or dative 209
present tense 111, 118-9, 124
present participle 16, 117
present subjunctive 114, 122, 126
prices 220
pro 196
pronouns 16, 25, 37-8, 86-108
proper names 59-60
punctuation 150, 240-1
put 245-6

quantity 219
questions 16, 233-6
quotation marks 240-1

reflexive 16
reflexive pronouns 91
reflexive verbs 159-61
relative clauses 103-6
relative pronouns 103-6

same 28-9
sämtlich 102
Saxon genitive 59
seasons 21, 223
sein (pronoun) 37, 92
sein (verb) 118-123, 132-3
seiner 86
seit 90, 212
seitdem 138, 212
selbst 91
sentence structure 228-237
separable verbs 124, 135-6
separable prefixes 135-6
setzen 246
sich 92, 159-61

sie 86
Sie 86
singular 17
sobald 212
so daß 212
solche 30, 66
sollen 124-7, 155
somebody, someone 92
sondern 211
sonst 211
sowie 210
sowohl ... als auch 211
statt 149, 208
stecken 246
stellen 246
stem 17
strong verbs 118-24, 166-71
subject 228
subjunctive 17, 114-5, 122-3, 127-8
subordinate clauses 134-5, 230
subordinating conjunctions 212-3
subtraction 219
such 30
suffixes 78-9
superlative 17, 74-6, 85
superlative adjectives 74-6
superlative adverbs 85

tausend 214
tense 17, 111-30
than 84
that 30, 103
that (conjunction) 212
the 18
there is/there are 243-4
this 30
till 194
time 82, 221-2
times of the day 21
towns 63-4
transitive verbs 131
translation problems 138-48
trotz 90, 209
trotzdem 211
tun 246

254 INDEX

über 165, 203
übers 198
Uhr 221-2
um 165, 196
umlaut 48-50
umlaut 19
um so 84
um ... willen 208
um ... zu 149
und 210
uninflected indefinite pronouns 95-100
uns 86
unser 37, 86
unsereiner 94
unter 165, 204-5
unters 198
use of tenses 137-71

ver- 135
verbs 17, 109-188
verb stem 17
verbs in -den/-ten 111
verbs in -eln, -ern 111
verbs in -ieren 117
verbs in -sen, -ßen, -xen, -zen 111
verbs followed by prepositions 163-5
verbs taking the dative 162-3
verbs with two accusative objects 163
viel 101
viertel 221
voice 17, 110
vom 19
von 165, 192-3
vor 165, 205-6
vors 19
vowel change 119

während 90, 208, 212
wann 233, 248
warum 233
was (pronoun) 104-5
was (interrogative) 233

was für 235-6
weak nouns 56
weak verbs 111-7
weder ... noch 211, 231
wegen 90, 209
weil 212
welch 233
welche 30
wem 107, 233
wen 233
wenig 95, 102
wenn 142-3, 247
wer 107, 233
werden 113, 115, 120
wessen 107, 233
what 233
what kind of 233
when 212, 233, 247-8
which 233
who 107, 233
whom 233
whose 233
why 233
wider 90
wie 213, 233
wieder- 136
wir 86
wissen 129-30
with 191
without 196
wo 105-6, 233
woher 233
wohin 233
wollen 124-5
word order 81-3, 108, 210-1, 228-30
worüber 104
würde 115-6, 143

yes 237
you 86

zehn 214
zer- 135
-zig 214

zu 149-50, 165, 193
zum 19
zur 19
zwei 214-5
zwischen 206

HARRAP'S GERMAN STUDY AIDS

Also available in this series

GERMAN VOCABULARY

★ Ideal revision aid
★ Particularly suitable for GCSE
★ 6000 vocabulary items in 65 themes

142mm × 96mm/256pp/plastic cover
ISBN 0 245-54630-8/£1.95

GERMAN VERBS

★ Over 200 verbs fully conjugated
★ Index of 2400 common verbs
★ Notes on verb constructions

142mm × 96mm/256pp/plastic cover
ISBN 0 245-54629-4/£1.95

MINI GERMAN DICTIONARY

★ Handy format
★ Sense distinctions clearly indicated
★ High information content

142mm × 96mm/640pp/plastic cover
ISBN 0 245-54573-5/£1.95